MW00426605

20 Concepts for Care
Essays on Infant/Toddler Development and Learning

EDITED BY
J. Ronald Lally, Peter L. Mangione,
and Deborah Greenwald
PITC (Program for Infant/Toddler Care)

Copyright © 2006 WestEd. All rights reserved. No part of this publication may be reproduced or distributed in any form or by any means, or stored in a database or retrieval system, without the prior written permission of the publisher.

ISBN-13: 978-0-914409-39-7
ISBN-10: 0-914409-39-5
Library of Congress Control Number: 2006933089

This book was printed on acid-free recycled paper.

....

We gratefully acknowledge the following people for their contributions to this publication: Joan Weaver, editorial support; Christian Holden, layout, design, and photography; and Sara Webb-Schmitz and Sheila Signer, photography.

....

WestEd, a nonprofit research, development, and service agency, works with education and other communities to promote excellence, achieve equity, and improve learning for children, youth, and adults. WestEd has 14 offices nationwide and also serves the states of Arizona, California, Nevada, and Utah as one of the nation's Regional Educational Laboratories.

For more information about WestEd:

> http://www.WestEd.org
> 415.565.3000 or 877-4-WESTED

> WestEd
> 730 Harrison Street
> San Francisco, CA 94107-1242

The Program for Infant/Toddler Care (PITC) seeks to ensure that America's infants get a safe, healthy, emotionally secure and intellectually rich start in life.

For more information about PITC:

> http://pitc.org
> 415.289.2300

> PITC
> WestEd
> 180 Harbor Drive, Suite 112
> Sausalito, CA 94965-1410

Contents

Foreword

This publication presents current thinking in the field of infant/
toddler development and care. Leading experts in infant/toddler
development have contributed essays drawn from research, theory,
clinical case studies, and carefully documented practice. Each essay
represents the perspective, voice, and professional expertise of the
individual author. Rather than being comprehensive, the essays
focus on specific ideas or issues. Some papers summarize research
or theory while others offer insights from early care and education, early intervention, or infant mental health practice. All of them
provide a springboard for reflection, discussion, and further exploration, especially for infant/toddler professionals seeking to enhance
their programs and for students in the early care and education field.

We are honored to be able to present the work and thinking of some
of the field's most influential minds. We hope you will find much to
consider and enjoy.

J. Ronald Lally
Peter L. Mangione
Deborah Greenwald

Being Held in Another's Mind

By Jeree Pawl, Ph.D.

What does it mean to be held in another's mind? Why does it matter, and how does such a feeling develop? Everything that we know about babies leads to the conclusion that they seek human connection, not only to survive but for its own sake. They are born looking for us. Given a choice of what to look at in their first hours, it is always the human face they choose.

Babies begin to put their worlds together immediately. All of the rich sensations they have are recorded in their bodies, their feelings, and their brains. Just from the natural feedback from her body, a baby becomes aware of being a "doer" (a waving arm) and of being "done to" (lifted, touched). All of the images, sounds, sensations, and smells of each caregiving experience commingle — and they remain with the baby even when she is alone and resting. Repeated experiences evoke memories, and they blend with immediate sensations; gradually, as these experiences accumulate, a sorting occurs and begins to create order. The baby begins to anticipate: a snapping sound, a light, a voice, then food. The hungry baby now stops crying when he hears only the sound. He grows increasingly able to anticipate, react, join in mutual feelings and turn-taking, and attend with someone to things in the world, like books, toys, or a panting puppy.

But sometime around seven to nine months, something new is happening. The baby's mother points at something and, instead of staring fixedly at her mother's hand, the baby looks where her mother is pointing. Soon the baby — who frequently has stretched out her hand towards something that is out of reach, grunting as she strains — points instead. She turns to look to see if her mother gets the idea. She does. The baby has made the discovery that her mother has a mind! The child can now have the intention to affect someone's mind and to be a reader of minds. The baby now knows her wishes and intentions can be in someone else's mind. The powerful wish to know and be known becomes more possible. This is a complex achievement that emerged from the child's experiences. All along this child has felt noticed, responded to, and has been aware of her impact in the moment and over time.

In most circumstances there is an ongoing development of the sense of being held by another — a sense of continuousness. Responsiveness in caring creates this sense over time. A baby sits contentedly with her back toward her parent for a long time, absorbed in play with small cups. For the baby, there are sensations, cues, and memories of all kinds that are part of this one occasion. A child feels safe and contained when those cues and memories evoke a sense of being with someone that is positive. This feeling will persist even when she is alone in her crib. She carries it with her — this sense of nurturance, of the parents' presence even in absence, and her existence for them. She is held in the parents' mind. This feeling continuously deepens.

However, there are some parents to whom a child exists so peripherally that the child has needed to do most of the adapting. He has been attended to only around the edges of the adults' schedule and concerns. He is often missing from their awareness — rarely held in mind. A baby with so little voice in what his experiences are has little sense of impact and little sense of even knowing what he needs or wants. His sense of being with another is impoverished.

When a parent is too-much missed, too-long absent, the child is overcome by yearning and sadness. Images, feelings, and memories usually so assuring provoke, increasingly, unhappiness and despair. It is not that the image of the mother is not maintained but that the comforting image of mother is overwhelmed and replaced with feelings of anxiety and loss. The child no longer feels held, but abandoned. The sense of safety, containment, and continuity is lost.

This is extremely relevant to child care centers and family child care homes. Some children arrive as small infants. In these circumstances the teachers who care for the baby play very similar and complementary roles to the parent. Yet the relationship is not the same because the feelings a parent has for a child are different from the feelings a teacher or caregiver has for the child. The meaning of the child is different to each. The teacher would not feel the same connection to and passion for the child that the parent does. The child is fully equipped to feel and respond to this very important difference. The sun beams down on her when her adoring parent smiles. Other smiles, like the smiles of her teacher, will be just a very, very nice day.

But the issue is the same in regard to the child's need to be noticed, appreciated, attended to, and to feel effective. With this necessary responsive care, the teachers, too, will become an assuring, containing, and continuous presence. The child receives from the teacher what she needs to maintain her sense of connection to the parent in the parent's absence.

Toddlers and preschoolers, whether they have had long experience in care or have just begun, have the same need. They need help not only with being reassured of their parents' whereabouts and existence but also with reassurance that they exist for their parents. Often we quite properly remind children that their parents are somewhere and that they will surely come — that their parents are not lost to them. As important, however, is helping children with the fear that their parents have lost them.

A child's sense of being held in the mind of a parent is supported and confirmed if there has developed a parallel sense that he exists in that way for the teacher. The teacher notices, sees, and responds. The child exists for the teacher when he is not immediately with her. He feels that strongly, through his sense of being seen and known. The teacher conveys this sense to him by understanding and knowing him, by reading his mind and behavior, by perceiving a need and offering something to him before he had directly indicated that he wanted it, by remembering what the child likes and dislikes and what they have done together. These things create, in a child, this important sense of his being in the mind of the teacher.

In the parents' absence, helping the parents exist for the child and helping the child know she also exists for the parents are important aspects of good care. There are many concrete and imaginative ways to do this. For example, a teacher says, "Mommy is getting all her papers and going to the bus — she'll be here soon," or, "Daddy is wondering right this minute what you are doing," and this is elaborated. Still, it is the quality of the teacher's relationship with the child that is the guarantee that these important feelings can be sustained. To be a part of a process so vital to a child is a wonderful privilege. To be held in another's mind is a precious thing. Equally precious is to hold another in one's own.

Metatheories of Childrearing

By J. Ronald Lally, Ed.D.

Every single adult, whether conscious of it or not, has an overarching theory that drives his or her childrearing practices. This organizing — or "meta" — theory greatly influences how each of us relates to and cares for children. Simply put, one's metatheory is the story carried in one's head about what drives children to action and how children should be treated. A metatheory of childrearing has two parts. The first part contains one's beliefs about young children: *"This is who children are. This is how they are made up. This is what motivates them. This is how they function."* The second part of the theory is based on the first part and is a kind of action plan for adult/child interactions: *"If children are as I believe them to be, then to be a responsible adult I must treat them in ways that are consistent with their nature."*

A number of competing metatheories of childrearing are popular with caregivers, parents, and policymakers in the United States today. Some have a long history and others are relatively new. I describe them in broad strokes below, so that you will be aware of the various beliefs people hold about how young children function. Because the vision of a child that one holds dictates what is seen as proper and appropriate childrearing behavior, those beliefs shape one's childrearing strategies. Often differences of opinion about strategies for childrearing occur between a child development professional and a client, parent, or trainee. Many times this difference is caused not because of a lack of information but rather because information that does not fit one's metatheory is rejected. To be effective in our work, we not only have to share the latest research theory about who children are and how they grow, but we also need to acknowledge and relate to the strong and sometimes unacknowledged theories that are held by those engaged in childrearing — including ourselves.

I. Natural Unfolding / Noble Savage

This metatheory comes from the early writings of Jean Jacques Rousseau and influenced, to varying degrees, Pestalozzi, Dewey, and Neil. It views children as basically good souls that need to be protected from the damaging messages of society. The child is viewed as a blossoming flower — on a trajectory for healthy growth that is present from birth. From this metatheory, a child's development can be damaged by too much interference from the outside. The natural urges of the child do not have to be controlled or shaped, nor does the child need to be trained to live in harmony with others. It is the job of the adult to get out of the way of the natural growth process and allow for the child's unfolding — and not to try to shape the child's behavior to meet societal standards. This "nature gospel" of education was quite popular in the United States in the late 1960s and early 1970s and inspired pedagogical methods worldwide.

"I wish to wrest education from the outworn order of doddering old teaching hacks as well as from the new-fangled order of cheap, artificial teaching tricks, and entrust it to the eternal powers of nature herself, to the light which God has kindled

and kept alive in the hearts of fathers and mothers, to the interests of parents who desire their children grow up in favour with God and with men."

   – Johann Pestalozzi, quoted in Silber

II. Tabula Rasa / Blank Slate / Empty Vessel

The "blank slate" is another theory adhered to by many. The child is seen as coming into the world without predisposed inclinations. Starting with Aristotle and continuing with the writings of John Locke, this theory became popular in modern America through the writings of J.B. Watson, the father of American psychology, and in the late 1960s through the work of B.F. Skinner and the "behaviorist school." Many policymakers and politicians concerned to see that children obtain basic academic skills hold to this notion. From this point of view, the way a child turns out is completely based on the experiences the child has in the environment in which he or she is raised and from information provided by others. All things, including child motivation, are produced, shaped, and molded by those in control of the experiences to which the child is privy. Under this belief system, those raising a child shoulder immense responsibility for how intelligent the child will become, how the child will express himself or herself, and how the child will act in relation to others. Little credence is given to the concepts of temperamental differences, inborn intelligence, or biological predisposition. Motivation to learn is often seen as the responsibility of the adult and not innate to the child. Because how a child turns out is to the blame or praise of those who raise the child, it is the adult's role to "write" on the "blank slate" or "fill" the "empty" child early and often with good and useful things — as much of the right content as possible.

   "There is no such thing as innate ideas; there is no such thing as moral precepts; we are born with an empty mind, with a soft tablet (tabula rasa) ready to be writ upon by experimental impressions. Beginning blank, the human mind acquires knowledge through the use of the five senses and a process of reflection."

   – John Locke

III. The Tempted [Devil on the Left Shoulder – Angel on the Right]

Many people bring from their religious training a view of the child as a being who is constantly tempted by competing messages: to do evil or selfish things or to do good or selfless things. Adults with this metatheory want to help the child to be vigilant to and resist temptation so that he or she can live a good and productive life. A key role in child rearing, then, is to keep the child from falling victim to temptation. Adults work to keep the child from temptation and remind the child that he or she will be tempted to do bad things in a constant struggle between good and evil. These adults see their job as reinforcing the messages of the angel and reminding the child to resist the tempting messages of the devil.

"Be strong. The devil fights you. But this does not mean that you are sinful. Nor should his attacks shake you or confuse you.... Each time you repulse an attack of the devil you secure a victory and you gratify God.... Thus the temptations force the evil that is hiding in us to come to the surface. The temptations arise from the flesh, the world, and the devil."

– St. Theophan the Recluse

IV. Unsocialized Savage

This theory comes from Puritan writings and beliefs. From this point of view, unless impulses are strongly inhibited and controlled right from birth, the child will continue into adulthood as an unsocialized and uncivilized being. Early urges, if not checked, will create an adult who is too sexual, is unethical, and is greedy — someone who seeks only personal pleasure and gain. Thus, it is the duty of the responsible adult to control the child's willfulness and stifle acting-out urges with stern, powerful, and consistent discipline. This way of viewing the child leads adults to practices that are aimed at nipping expected bad behavior in the bud. Feeding on schedule, letting a child cry things out, not "spoiling," and clear messages of adult control are techniques often used by those who adhere to this theory. Childrearing is seen as a fight for power between child and adult right from the beginning of life. Therefore, adult control of child behavior should start as early as possible so that self-will can be broken and the child kept from a destructive developmental trajectory.

According to Philip Greven, the first of the Protestant temperaments — the "evangelical" — was exhibited by groups like the Puritans, the Baptists, and the Methodists. Evangelical parents, he writes, were obsessed by human sinfulness and so strove for complete authority over their children and used every means to "break the will" of youngsters. In adulthood, many children reared in such families surrendered any remnant of self-hood in a cathartic conversion experience, a final submission to a demanding deity — onto whom they projected parental characteristics.

> **– Philip J. Greven, The Protestant Temperament**

V. The Early Unformed

Many people look at infants and do not see anything but an eating, sleeping, and defecating machine. They see in the child no intellectual activity, no aware-ness of feelings, and little need for social contact. They believe that the child is not capable of conscious activity until he or she has grown out of the infancy period. Statements about childrearing from this point of view follow this pattern: "Why would anyone talk to infants, interact with them, consider their feelings — they can't understand you." The adult who be-lieves that the infant or young child has few feelings and does not register much about what's going on feels free to do most anything in the child's presence or to leave the child alone for long periods. Loud televisions, screaming fights within earshot, or isolation in a crib or playpen are seen as having no effect on the child because the child registers little. Pretty

much anything can happen (or not) with-out permanent consequence to the very young child. Many fathers who hold this metatheory delay relating to their child until the child is about two and seems to have developed sufficiently to demon-strably need or benefit from engagement.

In fact, the baby (for both Freud and Lacan) is a kind of blob, with no sense of self or individuated identity, and no sense even of its body as a coherent unified whole. This baby-blob is driven by NEED; it needs food, it needs comfort/safety, it needs to be changed, etc. These needs are satisfiable, and can be satisfied by an object. When the baby needs food, it gets a breast (or a bottle); when it needs safety, it gets hugged. The baby, in this state of NEED, doesn't recognize any distinction between itself and the objects that meet its needs; it doesn't recognize that an object (like a breast) is part of another whole per-son (because it doesn't have any concept yet of "whole person"). There's no distinc-tion between it and anyone or anything else; there are only needs and things that satisfy those needs.

> **– Dr. Mary Klages, Lectures on Jacques Lacan**

VI. The Innocent

In many cultures children are seen as innocent and unmotivated by inappropriate thoughts and feelings until they reach their fifth, sixth, or seventh birthday. This theory postulates that until reaching this "age of reason," the child should not be held responsible for right or wrong actions. Before reaching the age of reason, the child is seen as not having the developmental equipment to operate from manipulative motives. Adults who view the young child as an innocent often give the child free rein to explore, to choose how and with what to play, and to "be a child." Once the child reaches the age of reason, however, things change dramatically. Adults' expectations for responsible behavior shift suddenly, and so do discipline techniques and education practices. At this transition point, children are held accountable, and school becomes a much more serious business.

"The age of discretion both for confession and for communion is the age in which the child begins to reason, i.e., around the seventh year, either before or after. From that time begins the obligation of satisfying both the precept of confession and of communion."

– A Letter from the Vatican: March 31, 1977, First Penance, First Communion

VII. The Competent/Vulnerable Child

This theory, based on recent analyses of research on child growth and development, paints the young child as simultaneously wearing two hats — one that displays the child's vulnerability and one that shows the child's competence. This view sees the child coming into the world with a personal learning agenda and owning a brain that is genetically wired to seek meaning and learn language. The child is seen as biologically programmed to attach to, socialize with, and learn from those who care for him or her. This view sees the child as a curious and motivated learner trying to make sense of the world he or she is entering. While the child has skills, motivation, and curiosity genetically built in, at the same time the child is desperately dependent upon adults for nurturance, support, and security. Without this adult support, the child will flounder. This theory, the one currently most supported by research, defines the responsible adult role as one of providing nurturance and support for the vulnerable component of the child's makeup while at the same time facilitating and respecting the child's skills and competencies. The adult who raises children from this metatheory acknowledges the child's biological predispositions to both vulnerability and competence and assumes responsibility for providing physical and emotional security while following the child's lead as the child acts out his or her social, intellectual, and language learning agenda.

"All children are born wired for feelings and ready to learn.... Human development is shaped by the ongoing interplay among sources of vulnerability and sources of resilience.... Children are active participants in their own development, reflecting the intrinsic human drive to explore and master one's environment."

– Jack P. Shonkoff and Deborah A. Phillips (Eds.), **From Neurons to Neighborhoods**

I have listed only a few of the more commonly held metatheories of childrearing. I am sure that you could identify many more, including combinations of those listed above. In our field, we work with many people who may see children differently than we do. It is important for us to remember this truth as we share our insights and knowledge with others.

For adults to relate to infants and toddlers well, it is imperative that they come to understand what science has discovered about how children function and grow and also to better understand their own personal metatheory of childrearing. Unexamined beliefs about who children are and how they function permeate the behavior of many well-meaning adults. Unexamined, these assumptions often become the base for childrearing practice. We need to be more conscious of how our assumptions play out in our relationships with young children.

To end, I want to suggest an exercise. Think about the metatheory your parents used to raise you. Take several minutes to do this. What did they believe about your core? How did their beliefs manifest in their behavior toward you? Ask these same questions of your metatheory and those of the people you work with. It will help you to see how you and others view young children and feel you should relate to them.

The Emotional Basis of Intelligence

By Stanley I. Greenspan, M.D.

Intellectual growth as well as emotional growth depends on emotional interactions. Each interaction between a child and another person gives rise to feelings such as pleasure, annoyance, surprise, sadness, anger, curiosity, and so forth. Variations in the quality and intensity of these and other feelings make for an almost infinite variety of emotional patterns. As discussed in some detail in our books *Building Healthy Minds* and *The Secure Child* (Greenspan, 1999, 2002), these patterns go through six basic stages and three advanced ones. For example, at the first level, Self Regulation and Interest in the World, emotional interactions enable the infant to become interested in the pleasure of sights and sounds, or else there would be no reason to look and listen. At the second level, Falling in Love, emotional interactions become the basis for forming a relationship with caregivers (that is, the pleasure and delight in relating). At the third level, Purposeful Communication, they lead to two-way communication and the first sense of causality. The earliest sense of causality emerges not from sensorimotor explorations, as Piaget thought (Piaget, 1962), but from earlier emotional interactions, a smile causing a smile back (Greenspan, 1981, 1997a). At the fourth level, Beginning of a Complex Sense of Self, emotions lead to pattern recognition and shared problem solving (the beginning of scientific thinking). A toddler, for example, takes father by the hand and exchanges many emotional gestures through looking, vocalizing, and pointing, in pursuit of the emotional goal of finding mother. Interacting in a continuous flow of emotional problem-solving interactions also leads to a preverbal sense of self. The toddler connects his different problem-solving interaction patterns to form a sense of "me."

Pleasurable problem-solving interactions lead to communication becoming a goal in its own right — the goal of being close to another person through sharing gestures and then ideas. At the fifth and sixth levels, Emotional Ideas and Emotional Thinking, respectively, emerging words such as "mother" or "apple"

become invested with the emotional patterns that characterize the interactions of which they are a part. "Mother" is not simply a person with long hair. "Mother" equals warmth, protection, excitement, and bossiness. Similarly, an "apple" tastes good as well as being round and red. Over time, such complex emotional interactions enable the child to form symbols, give them meaning, and eventually build bridges between symbols. In this way, emotional interactions become the foundation for both emotional and intellectual growth and, more broadly, for intelligence (Greenspan, 1997b).

While emotional and social growth are not surprising outcomes of emotional interchanges, most people do not think of cognitive or intellectual abilities as stemming from these same interactive patterns — yet, they do. For example, how does a child learn to say "Hello"? Do the child's parents teach her this seemingly simple cognitive lesson by telling her to say "Hello" only to close friends, relatives, and those who live within a quarter-mile of her house? Or is the decision to say "Hello" mediated by an emotional cue, such as a warm feeling in her body as she sees a familiar, friendly face? If cognitive learning involves emotional cues, and we think it does, how would we promote it? We would promote it by creating opportunities for interactions in which the child could link her emotions, thoughts, and behaviors together.

Similarly, advanced intellectual activity requires emotional interactions. It involves two components: an emotionally mediated creation of personal experience and a logical analysis of that experience. This process begins early in development when children's earliest experiences are "double-coded" according to both their physical and emotional properties. For example, the ball is round and red — at the same time, it feels "good" and looks "exciting." The food is yellow and firm and simultaneously tastes "delightful" or "nasty." As a child learns about size, shape, and quantity, these experiences are also both emotional and cognitive in nature. For example, "a lot" is more than a child expects or "a little" is less than he wants. It follows, then, that the ability to count or formalize these quantities is simply a logical classification of what the child already "knows" emotionally. Similarly, when trying to understand a concept like "justice," an older child "knows" it through personal experiences of being treated fairly or unfairly on a personal level and then reflects on or analyzes this personal experience. Emotional interactions create the "experiences" that generate the ideas on which the child

can then reflect. Without such emotional interactions, thinking remains at a level of rote memory production rather than a creative and reflective process.

Supporting these early emotional interactions is, therefore, critical for intellectual and social growth. In fact, school literacy depends on a child's mastering of these essential thinking capacities that stem from early emotional interactions. They lead to the ability to attend, listen, follow directions, communicate ideas, participate in a group, understand what is heard or read, solve math problems, and, eventually, write meaningful words, sentences, and paragraphs.

Many educators and mental health professionals have believed that relationships — emotional and social growth — on the one hand, and intelligence and academic skills on the other, are separate lines of development. Many have further believed that there are trade-offs. Programs, therefore, tend to emphasize one or the other. In our books *The Growth of the Mind* and *The First Idea*, we have shown, however, that intellectual and emotional development stem from the same basic processes (Greenspan, 1997b; Greenspan and Shanker, 2003).

Overview: Six Stages of Functional Emotional Development
(Greenspan, 1999, 2002, 2003)

Functional Emotional Developmental Level	Emotional, Social, and Intellectual Capacities
Self Regulation and Interest in the World Shared attention and regulation *(from birth on)*	Pleasurable interest in sights, sound, touch, movement, and other sensory experiences. Leads to looking, listening, calming, and awareness of the outer world and simple patterns.
Falling in Love Engagement and relating *(from 2 to 4 months on)*	Pleasurable feelings characterize relationships. Growing feelings of intimacy.
Purposeful Communication Two-way intentional, emotional signaling and communication *(from 4 to 8 months on)*	A range of feelings become used in back-and-forth emotional signaling to convey intentions (e.g., reading and responding to emotional signals); the beginning of "cause and effect" thinking.
Beginning of a Complex Sense of Self Long chains of coregulated emotional signaling, social problem solving, and the formation of a presymbolic self *(from 9 to 18 months on)*	A continuous flow of emotional interactions to express wishes and needs and solve problems (e.g., to bring a caregiver by the hand to help find a toy). a. Fragmented level (little islands of intentional problem-solving behavior). b. Polarized level (organized patterns of behavior express only one or another feeling state, e.g., organized aggression and impulsivity; or organized clinging, needy, dependent behavior; or organized fearful patterns). c. Integrated level (different emotional patterns — dependency, assertiveness, pleasure, etc. — organized into integrated, problem-solving emotional interactions such as flirting, seeking closeness, and then getting help to find a needed object).

Functional Emotional Developmental Level	Emotional, Social, and Intellectual Capacities
Emotional Ideas Creating representations, symbols, or ideas *(from 18 months on)*	Experiences, including feelings, intentions, wishes, action patterns, etc., are put into words, pretend play, drawings, or other symbolic forms at different levels. a. Words and actions are used together (ideas are acted out in action, but words are also used to signify the action). b. Somatic or physical words are used to convey feeling state ("Tired legs," "Head hurts"). c. Action words are used instead of actions to convey intent ("Hit you!"). d. Feelings are conveyed as real rather than as signals ("I'm mad," "Hungry," "Need a hug" as compared with "I feel mad," or "I feel hungry," or "I feel like I need a hug"). In the first instance, the feeling state demands action and is very close to action; and in the second one, it's more a signal for something going on inside that leads to a consideration of many possible thoughts and/or actions. e. Global feeling states are expressed ("I feel awful," "I feel OK," etc.). f. Polarized feeling states are expressed (feelings tend to be characterized as all good or all bad).
Emotional Thinking Building bridges between ideas: logical thinking *(from 2 years on)*	Symbolized or represented experiences are connected together logically to enable thinking. This includes the capacity for the following: a. Differentiated feelings (gradually there are more and more subtle descriptions of feeling states — loneliness, sadness, annoyance, anger, delight, happiness, etc.). b. Creating connections between differentiated feeling states ("I feel angry when you are mad at me") and logical thinking ("The letters 'C,' 'A,' and 'T' spell CAT").

These basic stages of functional emotional development lead to a number of advanced stages of intelligence and thinking, including the following:

a. **Multicausal thinking** *(from 4 to 5 years on)*

b. **Gray-area, differentiated, and comparative thinking** *(from 7 to 8 years on)*

c. **Thinking of an internal sense of self and internal standard (i.e., judgment)** *(from 10 to 12 years on)*

Creativity, Shared Meaning, and Relationships

By Carlina Rinaldi

The search for meaning begins from the moment of birth, from the child's first silent "why," and continues all through life. It is a difficult search. Young children make enormous efforts to put together often-disconnected fragments of experience to make sense of things. They persevere with their search stubbornly, tirelessly, making mistakes, and often on their own. But while engaged in this search, children ask us to share the search with them. We as teachers are asked by children to see them as scientists or philosophers searching to understand something, to draw out a meaning, to grasp a "piece of life," and to respect this search as a quality central to all human beings. We are asked to be the child's traveling companion in this search for meaning. We are also asked to respect the meanings that children produce, the explanatory theories they develop, and their attempts to find and give answers. When we honor children this way, the children reveal themselves to us: We come to know how they perceive, question, and interpret reality, and to understand their relationships with it.

I believe that teachers must communicate a willingness to assist children in their search for meaning in life. Two of the most important questions we have to ask ourselves as teachers are

✣ "How can we aid young children in their search for the meaning of things, and the meaning of life itself?"

✣ "How can we respond to their constant questions, their 'whys' and 'hows,' with eyes that don't see them as helpless or unknowing, but rather with eyes that acknowledge the quest to learn and to know?"

The important thing for teachers to do to support the child's quest is, first, to view the child as competent for the task and, second, to subjectively engage with the child in his or her pursuits. Look at children as avid seekers of meaning and significance and as producers of interpretive theories. Looking and listening with love, complicity, and openness allows teachers to understand what lies behind the child's questions and theories.

The intention on the part of children to produce questions and search for answers is the genesis of creativity. The behaviors that teachers exhibit toward the child's intention to search, the process of searching, and the conclusions a child reaches either support or dampen creativity. The teacher's job is to engage in a "relational creativity" with the child that both revels in the child's creativity and stimulates the teacher's own creativity to find ways to help the child observe, analyze, interpret, and build theories.

Sometimes these theories, these explanations that children produce, are wonderfully sweet: "It's raining because the man on TV said it was going to rain," or, "It's raining because God is crying." By honoring rather than correcting these answers, and by inventing ways to help the child pursue his questions further, a teacher does her part in the creative process. This often means slowing down and giving greater significance to the child's stopping to study a flower for ten minutes, her enchantment with rain on a window, and her various wonderings than most adults might normally do. It takes time to produce interpretive theories and come up with answers. It takes time to study. This need for time must be respected.

Theory building also builds relationships because it is predicated on a search for common meaning. Communication of theories between child and teacher or child and child transforms the young child's world from one that is intrinsically personal into one that is shared. The child sees his knowledge shared by another, and this sharing of theories is a key component of easing a child's feelings of uncertainty and solitude.

When teachers "open up" to children and really listen to the child's creations, not only in the physical sense but also in the metaphorical sense, they endorse creativity. They listen and give value to differences and make room for the points of view of others. Listening is the foundation of every learning relationship. Unfortunately, there are schools that do not listen in this way because they have a curriculum to follow and they try to correct "mistakes" immediately — to provide quick solutions to a problem and not give

children the time to find their own solutions. What gets lost is creativity.

Children are biologically predisposed to communicate and establish relationships; this is why we must always give them plentiful opportunities to represent their mental images and to be able to represent them to others. Teachers must realize not only that the other is indispensable to the child's developing sense of identity but also that learning with others generates pleasure in the group and makes the group become the place of learning. This, then, is the revolution that we have to put into place in child care. Through "relational creativity" children develop a natural sensitivity toward creating ideas, appreciate and codevelop ideas with others, and share common meaning. This is why I consider the learning process to be a creative process.

Creating Responsive, Reciprocal Relationships with Infants and Toddlers

By Peter L. Mangione, Ph.D.

In our work with the Program for Infant/Toddler Care (PITC), we consider responsiveness to be at the heart of positive, nurturing relationships with infants and toddlers. Our definition of responsiveness corresponds to that of Marc and Helen Bornstein (1995) and includes three elements: contingency, appropriateness, and promptness. Contingency means that the adult nurturer's actions occur in response to the baby's behavior or cues. By appropriateness, the Bornsteins suggest that the adult's response meets the child's need or fits with the child's interest. Promptness, of course, means that the adult's response follows shortly after the child's behavior or cue. However, for those responses that are under the adult's conscious control, promptness does not mean a hurried or rushed response. Responses that occur at a pace the infant can attend to support the development of reciprocal or back-and-forth interaction between the baby and the adult.

The definition of responsiveness raises a critically important question for the infant/toddler field: How can we help infant care teachers or caregivers respond to infants contingently, appropriately, and promptly? PITC's answer to this question centers on the "Responsive Process," which infant care teachers can use to increase their responsiveness to babies. This process consists of three steps: Watch, Ask, and Adapt. It starts with watching or observing the infant or toddler. Giving empathetic attention while providing care opens up the possibility of deepening one's understanding of an individual child's behavior and cues. Observation thus enables adults to follow the child's lead and respond contingently and promptly. The "ask" step helps adults avoid giving rapid responses and over-stimulating babies; it instead leads them to explore the meaning of children's behavior moment by moment. It puts adults in the role of researchers who are trying to discover how to respond appropriately. The search for an appropriate response that meets the baby's need flows into the "adapt" step. The attempt to adapt to the baby may or may not meet the child's need. The adult's search for an appropriate response continues until one is found. In effect, the responsive process supports the development of attunement between the adult and baby, and it contributes to positive relationship experiences for the child.

But attunement with a baby is not achieved simply through a process of watching, asking, and adapting. When we observe responsiveness in action, we see harmonious interactions between adults and babies. Infant care teachers convey peacefulness and a sense of ease and emotional security through the calm pace with which they relate to children, the tone of their voices, the openness of their facial expressions, and the quiet attentiveness of their hands. Adults communicate so much to babies through their eyes, voices, and hands. The hands, in particular, can convey warmth, affection, and respect — a sense of peace. Leboyer's (1975) words come to mind:

> The hands that touch the child reveal everything . . .
> The child knows if the hands are loving
> In attentive and loving hands, a child abandons self, opens up
> We must let our hands lie on the child motionless.
> Not hands that are inert, perfunctory, distracted
> But hands that are attentive, alive, alert, responsive to the slightest quiver
> Hands that are light. That neither command or demand. That are simply there.

Learning to communicate calm, attentive regard to a child in a predictable way takes time. As Magda Gerber reminds us in a PITC video (1988), we have to unlearn what we think we should be doing and learn a new way of being with the infant. But does the need to learn to communicate responsively mean that we have to give up being spontaneous with babies? Hanuš and Mechthild Papoušek (1987) suggest otherwise. In reviewing a large body of psychobiological research on parent-infant interaction, the Papoušeks describe how infants and adults have biologically built-in responses to one another, for example, the greeting response. When a young infant raises her eyebrows and opens her eyes widely, the adult will intuitively or spontaneously do the same within a fraction of a second. There are many other examples of spontaneous responses to infants. These inborn responses provide the foundation for the intuitive care of an infant. Although intuitive responses are biologically based, they may be inhibited or absent in some adults. A psychological disturbance in the adult, in particular clinical depression, negative relationship experiences, or a tendency to "think too much," may interfere with the adult's inborn responses to infants. The concern about adults thinking too much resonates with Gerber's comment (PITC, 1988): "You have to unbusy your head and unbusy yourself."

Yet, increasing one's responsiveness with babies requires focused awareness and thought. The challenge for all adults responsible for caring for infants is to learn techniques such as the responsive process while continuing to be spontaneous and intuitive during interactions. Anna Tardos (personal communication, March 8, 2005) indicated that the Pikler Institutue in Budapest, Hungary, addresses this balance in training nurses (caregivers). Once nurses internalize the Pikler technique, their interactions with babies become natural and spontaneous. The technique — the way one picks up, holds, feeds, changes, and washes the baby — is prescribed or choreographed, so to speak. But some things are never prescribed — for example, eye contact, smiling, or caressing a child.

The Pikler approach also specifies how the nurse uses language with the child. The first level is prescriptive. It consists of telling the baby what will happen next in the sequence of care. However, the second and third levels are not prescribed. The second level is about what happened and what will happen in a general sense. This level includes the nurse acknowledging what the child is doing. At the third level, the nurse expresses emotion as an adult, which Tardos believes provides an emotional mirror for the infant. The second and third levels are always novel, for each situation and every moment with the baby are unique. The nurse integrates the communication techniques into a natural, spontaneous way of interacting with babies.

The need to be responsive to novelty and spontaneous with infants suggests that trying to teach them specific concepts or skills would be counterproductive. Indeed, in the language development domain, Hart and Risley (1995) did not observe instances of intentional teaching in their study of ways in which parents foster early vocabulary growth. Rather, they observed that "talking was laid onto social interaction" (Risley, 2005). In commenting on how adults used "extra talk" with babies, Risley (2005) described it as

> …capitalizing on the teachable moment to expand and elaborate your child's comment or words. That's where the best teaching happens. It always turns out that's an automatic part of extra talk…. It's automatically there if you're talking about extra things that are not business.

Responsively following the child's lead and offering expansions based on the child's present interest provide rich learning experiences. Adults possess the intuitive capacity to be responsive to babies verbally as well as nonverbally. To draw on this capacity, adults need to be intentional about opening themselves to developing a passionate interest in the children in their care. With such an interest, adults can become keen observers of development, sensitive to infants' cues and behavior, responsive to their needs, and better able to follow infants' lead and help them engage in expansive learning experiences.

A passionate interest in a young child stems from an emotional connection. Human relationships are emotional and reciprocal. Two adults in a relationship stabilize and regulate each other emotionally (Lewis, Amini, and Lannon, 2000). Although still reciprocal, a relationship between an adult and an infant differs from one between two adults. Babies are completely dependent on adults for emotion regulation (Siegel, 1997), but at the same time infants have an emotional impact on adults. At a very basic level, the baby affects the way the adult self-regulates as the adult guides emotion regulation for the baby. As an attachment develops between the infant and the adult, their reciprocal emotional connection provides the foundation for the sharing of novel, creative, and lively learning experiences.

Carlina Rinaldi (2001), of the Reggio Emilia schools in Italy, makes a compelling case that our image of the child greatly influences our interactions and relationships with children. There are different images of the child in our society, and sometimes one image may dominate over others. When this happens, many people may adopt the dominant societal image as their personal image. A commonly held image in our society today is that our relationships with children are mainly about power. In this view, either the adult wins or the child wins. It follows that effective childrearing requires the adult to assert or exercise power. The corresponding image of the child includes the following elements:

✤ someone who has to be motivated and directed to learn;

✤ someone who needs to be controlled; and

✤ someone whose interests or desires are in conflict with the adult's interests, desires, and expectations.

Needless to say, the image of the baby presented in this essay differs greatly from the above image. In responsive, reciprocal relationships, the adult relates to the child in ways that reflect the following image:

✤ someone who is competent — an active, motivated learner;

✤ someone who looks to the adult for nurturance and guidance; and

✤ someone who is capable of cooperating in a relationship with an adult and who thrives when given the opportunity to do so.

With this image, rather than focusing on power differences that are present in relationships between adults and infants, we focus on being responsive and engaging in reciprocal exchanges or nonverbal and verbal dialogue — dialogue at a pace that invites the child to take the lead, dialogue that is not intrusive but gives the child time and space to solve problems, dialogue that communicates respect, dialogue in which we share attention and meaning with the child, dialogue that communicates a genuine interest in the child, dialogue that helps the child to become emotionally secure, and dialogue that facilitates the child's active engagement in learning.

Nurturing Very Young Children Who Experience More Than One Language

By Barbara Zurer Pearson, Ph.D., with Peter L. Mangione, Ph.D.

Although experiences during the early years may vary tremendously, the foundation for learning language is the same for every child. Whether a child is learning one language or more than one, to foster language learning *from the earliest ages,* infant/toddler care should emphasize *warm, nurturing, one-on-one conversation that is responsive to the child's attempts to communicate.*

Learning in Any Language

The variety of experiences children have learning language in infant/toddler care is very great. For example, some children experience one language at home and another in child care; some experience two different languages at home and a third in care; and some experience the same language at home and in care. Whether children will eventually speak one language, two languages, or more, their earliest lessons take place in the universal language of human interaction. Well before the age when babies understand a word or two in the flow of language around them, caregivers teach babies important lessons about language.

1. Communicating and sharing emotions.

Babies show us from the beginning that soothing words and lullabies can calm them. We can also see the interest babies have in our words when they turn their heads toward us and watch our mouths and eyes. Research tells us that the mouth and eyes are the most important points of focus when babies gaze at the faces looking at them (Fantz ,1958; Johnson and others, 1991).

2. Building knowledge about language from familiar experiences.

At birth, a baby can distinguish her mother's voice, the one she has been hearing during the last 12 or so weeks of gestation (Shelov, 1994). Research shows that young infants naturally "tune in" more often and more consistently to people who speak the same language as their mother (Bosch and Sebastian-Galles, 2001). Though newborns can distinguish the phonemes of every language, by age one they are already much more sensitive to the sounds present in the languages they hear every day.

3. Putting pointing and talking together.

By six to nine months of age, babies know to look where our eyes are looking, and they will follow our pointing if it is in their field of vision. When they, too, learn to coordinate their pointing with a vocalization (McCune and others, 2003), they get us to name the things in their environment for them. Even if babies do not remember or cannot reproduce what we say, our words teach them the crucial lesson that things and actions in the world have names.

4. Taking turns.

Babies learn the rules for turn-taking and coordination with others in the context of vocalizing. We can speak with them gently from the moment they are born, but they generally start "answering" in their cooing at around three months if we give them time and encouragement to respond to us. This early back-and-forth communication will become the game of conversation and socialization more generally that children need to guide them toward the sentences and stories of their language. (The) stories help them progress beyond "learning language" to "learning through language" and eventually learning through schooling and their community's culture.

5. Following the babies' lead. Turn-taking goes an important step further when we use the babies' spontaneous sounds as the base for our turn. Letting the child lead helps us know the right place to start. If we build on the baby's babbles in how we respond to the child, we are more likely to be aiming our "lesson" at the right level, at the level where the child is and from which she or he can go forward. Research studies have shown that child-initiation will remain the key to child progress through the preschool years (Cross, 1977; Burns, 1992).

Nurturing and Communicating with Children Who Experience More Than One Language

At the foundation of nurturing infants and toddlers in the child care setting is respecting and honoring the concerns and wishes of the child's family. In working with the family, infant care teachers must balance three important considerations when trying to support children who are learning more than one language:

- ✥ enhancing babies' comfort and self-awareness with *continuity* between the home and the child care setting;

- ✥ encouraging caregivers to speak the language they speak most naturally;

- ✥ communicating in the language of the broader community, especially in settings in which there is great diversity in the home languages of the children.

For infants, each of these considerations is important. They are balanced differently from one setting to another, and, depending on the balance, one or two of these considerations may require extra attention.

1. Continuity. Because early learning, including communication and language, is integrated and influenced by the infant's sense of emotional security and comfort, babies should be provided with predictable routines that emphasize the continuity between the home and child care setting. The home language in the child care setting can help a child feel emotionally secure. For example, when an infant is having trouble settling down at naptime, having someone who can sing quietly with the child, right in her ear in her home language, may be helpful. The intimacy of the care and the familiarity of the rhythms and sounds of the home language help the child calm down and peacefully fall asleep. Using the home language also fosters the child's sense of self as a member of the family and its community and maintains strong ties, especially between the generations in the child's home.

2. Native language of the caregiver.

When caregivers speak their own native language, they can use the full range of rhythm and tone of voice to convey both *meaning* and *attitude* through their utterances. Native speakers also provide the best language models for children's language learning. It is advisable to have caregivers speak their best language, as long as communication with the rest of the staff can be maintained.

However, if it is necessary for some individuals to speak a language they speak imperfectly or with an accent, there is no lasting harm done to the child's language development, as long as there are other models available to the child as well (Pearson and Navarro, 1998; Baron-Cohen and Staunton, 1994).

3. The language of the broader community.

When the child's home language is not English, and no staff member speaks the child's home language (which is often the case in California), infant care teachers often wonder whether they should speak English or try to learn the child's home language. It is appropriate to communicate in a language different from the child's home language, as long as an effort is made to support the child when he tries to communicate in his home language. After all, many children worldwide are born into homes where two (or more) languages are spoken and where it is important for the child to become a functioning member of two or more language communities (Romaine, 1995).

Infant care teachers who are more competent in a language different from that of the broader community should use the language that is most natural to them at least some of the time. Research indicates that children with vastly different language experiences in early childhood settings can perform similarly in school. In a carefully balanced study of Hispanic schoolchildren in Miami (Oller and Eilers, 2002), when ten-year-old bilingual children who began learning English at age five were compared to bilingual children who began using English earlier, there were almost no differences between them in their fifth-grade reading and writing scores. The differences observed between the two groups' vocabulary at that age were more closely associated with the language of the home and appeared to depend less on the language of the school (English only versus Spanish and English equally). In other words, the home language was a stronger influence than the language of the school for some aspects of language, and the language of the school was a stronger influence for other aspects.

Program Models

Taking these three factors into consideration, we can picture several program models that maximize the language resources available.

Program Model 1: Caregivers speak child's language.

Child's language =	= Caregivers' language ≠	≠ Community language
Use the child's and caregivers' common language.		

Quality of the experience for infant or toddler:

✤ Continuity between the home and the child care setting, which supports the child's overall development and sense of self, and facilitates a secure relationship as the base for learning language.

✤ Caregivers speaking their own native language.

Key consideration:

�֍   Caregiver should frequently engage in warm, nurturing communication that is responsive to the child. This type of interaction provides a strong foundation for learning both a first and any additional languages.

Program Model 2: Caregivers speak community language.

Child's language ≠	≠ Caregivers' language =	= Community language
	Use the caregivers' and community language.	

Quality of the experience for infant or toddler:

✖   Caregivers speaking their own native language.

✖   Child has experience with community language.

Key considerations:

✖   The caregiver should frequently engage in warm, nurturing communication that is responsive to the child.

✖   Caregiver should work with the child's family to create continuity between the home and child care setting.

✖   Caregiver should support and value the child's efforts to communicate in the home language.

Program Model 3: Caregivers speak community language as a second language.

Child's language ≠	≠ Caregivers' language Caregivers' second language =	= Community language
		Use the community language.

Quality of the experience for infant or toddler:

✢ Child has experience with the community language.

Key considerations:

✢ If children of different linguistic backgrounds are in the same program, for example, the caregivers cannot speak four different languages natively, but the caregiver should still frequently engage in warm, nurturing communication that is responsive to the child.

✢ Caregiver should work with the child's family to create continuity between the home and child care setting.

✢ Caregiver should support and value the child's efforts to communicate in the home language.

✢ The program offers the child opportunities to interact with other adults who speak the community language natively.

Using the community language fosters a common language for the child care setting. In this circumstance, volunteers and family members who share the child's language can participate to enhance the continuity between the home and child care setting.

Program Model 4: Different caregivers use different languages (mixed).

Child's language =	= Some caregivers' language	Some caregivers' language =	= Community language
Use the child's language sometimes.			
	Use the community language sometimes.		

Quality of the experience for infant or toddler:

✤ Some continuity between the home and the child care setting, which supports the child's overall development and sense of self, and facilitates a secure relationship as the base for learning language.

✤ Caregivers speaking their own native language.

✤ Child has experience with the community language.

Key consideration:

✤ Caregivers should frequently engage in warm, nurturing communication that is responsive to the child.

Program Model 4 brings the benefits of the first two models, but it may introduce a greater administrative burden to coordinate caregivers who speak different languages.

From the child's point of view, there is little problem with using more than one language. The experiences of bilingual families show us different ways children adapt to the use of two languages (Baker, 2000). It is very common to have different people use different languages consistently, and children often come to expect it. Children as young as two have been known to protest when one person uses the language the children associate with another person, and they may insist that the person switch back to the customary language (Volterra and Taeschner, 1978; Baker, 2000). Other families use different languages in different settings — for example, one language in the home and another language outside the home (Deuchar and Quay 2000). In a child care setting, this may translate into using one language during intimate, one-to-one contact and another language in the group context. Of course, each program needs to work with families to determine the strategy that takes best advantage of the people and resources it has.

Summary

Infants and toddlers experiencing more than one language can learn language well in different kinds of child care settings. Some situations require special attention to ensure that they meet very young children's need for consistent, familiar routines that support their developing emotional security and sense of self. Providers should relate to infants and toddlers as conversational partners whose ideas and feelings they respect. This can be done in any language.

Stress, Nurture, and the Young Brain

By Megan Gunnar, Ph.D.

Stress has both physical and psychological triggers. Physically, stress is triggered by extreme heat, cold, illness, hunger, and the like. Psychologically, stress is triggered by expectations that bad things will happen or by emotional states (anger, fear) that throughout evolution are associated with threats to our physical well-being. When stress is triggered, our brain systems respond by turning up the activity regulating two important stress hormones, adrenaline and cortisol. These hormones coordinate a set of behavioral and metabolic changes that increase our chances of survival. However, turning up the stress system affects the way we develop. If we develop in environments that constantly trigger stress, we become highly sensitive to threat cues, are vigilant and attentive, and run or fight at the least provocation. These responses are mal-adaptive in safer environments because they can interfere with how well we attend in school; how easy we are to get along with; and how much at risk we are for developing stress-related disorders, both mental (such as anxiety, depression) and physical (such as cardiac disease). Adrenaline is hard to measure in young children because it requires collecting urine at specific times, and children are often not cooperative. Cortisol is relatively easy to measure in young children using small samples of saliva. In what follows, we describe what is known about the cortisol levels for children in child care.

Teachers have a powerful influence on children's stress hormones. Teachers can, of course, protect children so that the stress system is rarely triggered by physical risk. In addition, teachers can provide emotional support and protection so that children, even when they are frightened or angry, can gain solace and a sense of security from those who are caring for them.

Importance of Secure Relationships

Research shows that cortisol levels of children who are secure in their relation-ships with caregivers remain low, even when the children encounter situations that make them a little scared or angry. Secure relationships buffer the stress system and protect the brain from poten-tially damaging effects of elevated stress hormones. Babies gain security over time and individual by individual, as they ex-perience the reliability and sensitivity of each caregiver. When a baby knows that when he cries, gets scared, or frustrated, the adults he depends on will be there to protect and calm him, this knowledge keeps the hormones from escalating. Babies do not seem to transfer a feeling of security with one caregiver to a feeling of security with a different one, and it is very hard to develop trust without con-sistent caregiving arrangements.

Amount of Time in Child Care and Elevated Stress

Research has shown that in child care young children are vulnerable to produc-ing elevated stress hormone levels as the day wears on. Child care often challenges and taxes young children socially and cognitively. In part, this is why children can learn so much in high-quality child care settings. But, at the same time, because child care settings can be very challenging, children need consistent, secure relationships with providers to navigate these settings without triggering stress.

Three factors predict more stress hormone production in child care settings. The first is *age*. Toddlers appear to be the most vulnerable compared to children of other ages, perhaps because they have left the security of the infant room and now must navigate settings with more children and fewer providers. However, many three- and four-year-olds also show rising stress hormone levels over the child care day. *Temperament* matters, as both children who are more fearful and children who are more angry and aggressive produce higher stress hormone levels at child care. Finally, *quality* of care matters. Higher levels of stress hormone production are seen in lower-quality child care. Indeed, quality of child care appears to determine how much age and temperament matter. In child care of very high quality, there are only small differences in cortisol levels between younger and older children and between temperamentally difficult and easy children. As quality of child care decreases, age and temperament differences in stress become more marked.

Does Early Stress Lead to Later Problems?

Do young children who experience poorer-quality care from parents, guardians, and care providers develop stress systems that put them at risk for cognitive and emotional problems? Certainly we know that adverse early care is associated with a host of problem behaviors as children develop. There is ample evidence that poor-quality child care is not good for children, while high-quality child care can stimulate cognitive and social development. What we are less certain of is whether children who experience frequent elevations in stress hormones when they are young develop stress systems that contribute to the problems we associate with various types of adverse early care and neglect. Researchers using animals to model stress early in development have shown over and over that stress alters the way the brain develops. Animals who when young received less nurturance from their mothers or were deprived of nurturance as part of a study design produce more stress chemicals in their brains, are more fearful and reactively aggressive, learn more slowly and retain information less well, have difficulty in social interactions, tend to be pushed to the edge of social groups, and tend to occupy subordinate positions in the social hierarchy. Early experiences are not destiny. Researchers have also modeled enriching interventions that can alter these outcomes — although so far, with the interventions that have been tried, the animals still seem to carry evidence of early life stress experiences in their brains.

What we know less about is to what extent the animal models apply to human development. We do know that infants whose mothers are clinically depressed tend to receive more intrusive, erratic, and unresponsive care. This type of care is associated with higher stress hormone levels and brain wave patterns that mimic those seen in depressed adults. We also know that children whose mothers were depressed when they were young have higher cortisol levels at age four and that these higher levels predict that teachers will report more behavior problems when these children are in kindergarten and first grade. Moving to more extreme adverse early care, researchers know that children who are maltreated during their early years develop smaller brains that are organized somewhat differently than the brains of children who have not been maltreated. Maltreated children also produce higher levels of stress hormones. Thus, there is reason to believe that early experiences of stress do shape the brain and stress systems in humans, as has been shown in animals. As with animals, we can expect that interventions with stressed children can be effective in increasing their coping competence and resilience.

Conclusions from Research

These research findings, taken as a whole, should encourage continued attempts to reduce the burden of mental illness in parents of young children, to support intervention in situations of child maltreatment, and to improve the quality of child care that is available to young children and their families. They add to the evidence that poor-quality child care can be stressful and potentially detrimental to young children. These findings support continued attempts to promote policies that would provide high-quality child care to all families needing these services.

Nurturing Developing Brains, Minds, and Hearts

By Ross A. Thompson, Ph.D.

When the history of popular beliefs about childhood is written, the last years of the 20th century will be seen as an important turning point for two reasons. First, this was the period when discoveries about early brain development came to public attention. Drawing on years of research in cognitive neuroscience and developmental biology, the "I Am Your Child" campaign, launched in 1997, acquainted caregivers with the foundations of brain development during the first five years of life. Second, this was the period when school readiness became an important public and policy concern. When the National Education Goals Panel urged in 1997 that "all children shall enter school ready to learn," it focused attention on how the cognitive achievements of the preschool years provide a foundation for school success.

Taken together, these events helped to transform everyday thinking about early childhood development. Having always been viewed as a period of carefree play and warm, nurturant relationships, early childhood now became regarded as a period when the foundational achievements of brain and mental development establish lifelong potential and, thus, a "window of opportunity" for early stimulation.

Parents and teachers naturally sought to obtain guidance from brain research about how to ensure that infants and toddlers get a good early start. They received plenty of advice from the media, toy manufacturers, and even developmental scientists. Because brain development begins with a proliferation of neural connections followed by their selective retention, many caregivers concluded, for example, that it is important to provide rich, diverse stimulation in the early years to ensure that many neural networks are created, helping to ensure the brain's developmental potential. Indeed, the "use it or lose it" principle by which early experiences determine which neural connections are strengthened and which are lost convinced many caregivers that young children should be exposed to different languages, letters and num-

bers, and problem-solving challenges in an early developmental curriculum to ensure that relevant brain areas would be strengthened. The recommendation of the "I Am Your Child" campaign that parents should regularly talk, sing, and play with their young children fit well with the school readiness concerns that literacy, numeracy, and reasoning skills should be trained early. Not surprisingly, a small industry emerged to market toys designed to stimulate brain development, with provocative names like "Baby Einstein" to remind parents of their important responsibility to support brain development and thus give their offspring a good early start to school success.

Parents' and teachers' interest in enhancing early brain development is reminiscent of what Piaget used to call "the American question." He was regularly asked by parents in the United States: How can we use research on cognitive development to accelerate children's mental growth? Piaget argued that this was the wrong question to ask because mental development must unfold according to its own natural timetable. Beyond this, caregivers' desire to enhance cognitive competence and school readiness through enhanced early stimulation may be misguided unless it is based on a deeper understanding of how brains and minds develop in the early years. Indeed, when we consider carefully what research on early brain development and cognitive growth tells us about the young mind and its development, there are some new and surprising lessons to learn, with practical value.

Here are some of those lessons:

The developing brain is remarkably active, capable, and self-organizing. It grows through its own activity in everyday experience. When we think about cognitive growth, our intuitive metaphor is filling up a container (the mind) with information. Children's minds grow as they acquire greater knowledge and experience. But research shows that this metaphor is the wrong one for the developing mind. Young children's minds are not passive containers waiting to be filled; they are instead active organisms in pursuit of novelty and understanding. Neuroimaging studies confirm what experimental studies have shown: children do not wait for explanations to be provided; they strive to interpret experience in light of prior knowledge, spontaneously posing questions and drawing inferential conclusions — and mentally growing in this manner. "Use it or lose it" describes the importance of the brain's activity to strengthening neural networks, not only the need for external stimulation to provoke brain growth. Learning is not primarily a matter of imparting knowledge, but rather of the child's active construction of understanding from experience. No inorganic metaphor, even a computer, is adequate to portray the self-initiated activity and self-organization of early brain development.

Viewed in this light, what are the best experiential catalysts to the developing brain? Developmental research shows that they are most likely to occur in an infant's social interaction with a responsive adult. More than any toy, CD, or video, a sensitive social partner can respond appropriately to what has captured the child's interest (and is thus the stimulus of brain activity), provoke new interests and exploration, calibrate shared experiences to the child's readiness for new learning, and accommodate the child's unique temperamental qualities (which may, for some, require gradual rather than fast-paced stimulation). Sensitive social interaction simultaneously captures multiple senses in activity that is both predictable and unexpected, and it involves give-and-take that involves the child as an active, thinking participant. When parents and teachers interact with infants and toddlers in this relaxed, responsive manner, without a superordinate agenda or instruction to impart, they are likely to provide the kinds of experiences that stimulate the developing brain and mind.

Cognitive, social, and emotional development are deeply integrated in the developing brain. Despite the tendency of child experts to divide the developing child into domains of language, social, cognitive, and emotional development, or to refer to certain brain regions as the "language area" or "association area," brain functioning is far more deeply integrated and interconnected. Thinking, feeling, communicating, socializing, and other capacities draw on multiple interrelated brain areas. Brain structures primarily devoted to menory and thinking influence (and are affected by) structures primarily governing emotion and stress. The maturation of brain regions associated with self-regulation has simultaneous effects on the growth of attentional focus, reasoning strategies, and emotional self-regulation. It is thus

mistaken to consider developing thinking and reasoning skills without taking into consideration the influence of the young child's emotions or the social context within which cognitive growth occurs. This is especially apparent in the early years of life.

One reason why social interaction is so provocative of early brain growth is that it engages both the mind and the heart as infants and caregivers share new discoveries. Early learning is motivated by infants' emotions: their natural curiosity, their delight in confirming expectations about what will happen, their frustration at impediments to problem-solving, and the pleasure of achieving goals. These emotional dimensions of cognitive growth are enhanced by an adult's curious questioning, empathic pout, resonant sounds of effortful striving, and congratulatory applause. In later years, children's motivation to achieve and pride in accomplishment derives from parental evaluations of their performance. Viewed in this light, school readiness is both a matter of acquiring relevant cognitive skills and of developing the social and emotional readiness to benefit from learning experiences in classroom groups and other socially shared experiences. This reflects how mental development is deeply tied to the emotions and social experiences that energize new learning.

Chronic, uncontrollable stress is a hazard to the growth of minds and brains. The integration of young children's cognitive, emotional, and social experiences helps to explain why stress is such a potential hazard to early learning. As profiled by Megan Gunnar in this book, animal studies show that chronic early stress is associated with problems in social and emotional functioning and difficulties in learning and retaining information. Although much more research is needed to understand its effects in early childhood, there is accumulating evidence that chronic, uncontrollable stress can have similar effects with young children. This is especially concerning because of the vulnerability of young children's emotional lives. Developmental scientists have discovered that early childhood is not a period of carefree play for all children, and in troubled families young children sometimes show signs of depression, anxiety disorders, post-traumatic stress reactions, and the emergence of conduct disorders that reflect the impact of family stress. The same

children may have difficulties controlling their emotions and getting along with other children in child care settings, as well as having difficulties concentrating and learning.

High-quality learning environments for infants and toddlers look very different from high-quality educational programs for older children. In light of what we have learned about brain development and mental growth, it should not be surprising that the experiences that stimulate cognitive development will vary for children of different ages. By middle childhood, brain maturation ensures that children are capable of attentional and cognitive self-control, and this is reflected in their pleasure in mental challenges that can consume their interest for hours at a time. Children of this age can benefit from formal learning settings involving a teacher-driven agenda in which children work quietly for sustained periods by themselves on complex tasks. There has been a natural tendency to expect that such formal learning settings should be a model for educational environments for younger children as well. But research has confirmed that if young children are put into the kinds of formal classroom settings in which older children thrive, they become less interested in learning, expect less of themselves, and are more stressed and less cooperative. The reason is that their developing brains and minds require different kinds of learning environments. As reflected in research on developing brains and minds, these environments have the following qualities:

+ They are child-oriented rather than teacher-driven, building on the naturally emerging interests that motivate cognitive growth.

+ They provide young children with choices from among a variety of age-appropriate activities, capitalizing on the mind's activity as a spur to mental development.

+ They involve considerable social interaction between children as well as adult-child interaction because of the social catalysts to new learning and the benefits of a language-rich environment.

+ They include predictable routine and manageable demands, recognizing the incompatibility between chronic stress and intellectual discovery.

With the realization that developing brains and minds in the early years require support, research in developmental neuroscience and developmental psychology has provided helpful ideas for how to provide that support in homes and child care settings. The challenge for a wise society is to thoughtfully enlist that knowledge into caregiving practices that nurture brains, minds, and hearts of the next generation.

Play and Its Relationship to Preliteracy

By Edward Zigler, Ph.D.

A high-quality infant/toddler setting provides many opportunities for children to play and pretend and many materials to enable them to do so. In the following examples, Molly, Umberto, and Poonam are all engaged in what we would call language and literacy activities. Through play, they are learning symbol systems — language and writing — and also having fun.

✤ Molly, aged two years six months, is walking around her toddler classroom with a clipboard and a pencil. "I'm making a list," she declares importantly, and makes scribbling marks (which are different from the circles with legs she makes when drawing her family) on her pad. Molly has begun to understand that writing looks different from drawing.

✣ Umberto, aged two years, picks up a small suitcase, plops a hat on his head, and looking up questioningly says, "Keys?" Not finding any, he picks up a small wallet, crams it next to the play steering wheel, and waves, "Bye-bye, work." Umberto, remembering and recreating a going-to-work scenario, substitutes something else when he can't find the real keys — recognizing already that one thing can stand for another, a necessary skill when learning to associate sounds and letters.

✣ Poonam, aged eight months, is seated comfortably on her teacher Lola's lap on the floor looking at a picture book, while three other children lean over to listen and watch. Lola points to a picture of a cow, and spontaneously Poonam says, "Mmm" (probably remembering an earlier conversation when Lola read, "The cow says 'moo'"). Poonam, young as she is, has a rudimentary understanding that print has meaning — that the words in a book "say" something.

All of these experiences have taken place in the context of pleasure and play. There have been no worksheets or drills for these children. Nevertheless, these experiences have a profound and organic connection to the subject matter of reading and writing.

In order for such experiences and many more like them to occur, programs for young children must have well-qualified teachers who recognize the developmental capabilities of each child and the learning inherent in play. Play must be valued as the primary means by which children learn about their world. Teachers create meaningful, enjoyable learning opportunities as well as a safe and nurturing environment. Many varied opportunities for playful activity will ensure that children, through their normal daily activities, can exercise their curiosity, interest, and drive and sustain their inborn eagerness, ability, and passion to learn.

Advice for Teachers
Supporting Play in the First Three Years of Life

A Foundation for Emergent Literacy

Playing with babies and toddlers can be an important way to enhance emerging literacy. When children play, good things happen. We are not advocating teaching very young children to read, but we can help them, through play, develop the essential skills that are involved in later reading.

Birth through Year One

From birth on, talk to babies and repeat the sounds they make. This playful interaction becomes the basis for dialog and mutual communication. Surround them with sounds of music, singing lullabies, or nursery rhymes. The rhythm of sounds is soothing, and hearing is stimulated. Comment on noises, the water running, the barking of a dog, dishes or glasses clinking. When baby is able to sit up, read using hardcover books and point to pictures on the page. Even though the infant may not understand everything you say, books and words become familiar.

Years One to Two

Play games such as peek-a-boo and patty-cake. Using words repeatedly affords toddlers opportunities to hear them strung together with distinct sounds, allowing them to practice receptive language (when they try to repeat the words, they are practicing expressive language). Imitate sounds of familiar animals — cats, dogs, cows. The repetitions help toddlers discriminate sounds, essential for phonics. Continue to sing nursery rhymes and alphabet songs. Provide stacking and nesting games for play, which stimulate toddlers' perceptual skills and the recognition of shapes, colors, size, and direction. As you read to a toddler, ask questions to promote suspense; point to pictures and words on a page; change your voice, encouraging giggling and enjoyment; and ask questions and expand on the child's answers.

Years Two to Three

As they act out scripts of "birthday parties," "house," or "store," older toddlers learn sequencing and ordering of events, skills needed in later reading. Make-believe play involves practicing imagery, so necessary for story comprehension. Children learn new vocabulary and also how to form sentences when they play and take on different roles. These are abilities necessary for verbal fluency that later define the good reader. Using puppets and acting out stories provide opportunities to develop imagination. To further enhance the learning of phonemes, play rhyming games such as cat, rat, fat, sat, or ball, fall, small. Use three words in a row and ask a child which one does not belong, such as hat, old, pat; hit, car, sit; or rat, but, cat.

Teachers and Family Members: Talking Together

By Amy Laura Dombro, M.S.

Infants and toddlers need their caregivers and their family members to work together as partners. Together you can learn more about a child than either of you could alone. You can build a bridge of continuity between a child's world at home and at child care that helps her feel secure and connected to both places. You can figure out how best to meet a child's needs and nurture her skills and interests. But you can do these things *only* if you are talking to each other.

As a caregiver, pause a moment to consider:

- ⁕ How do you feel around children's family members?

- ⁕ How do you think they feel around you?

- ⁕ Have you ever talked with family members about your work together? Why or why not?

Here in the following example are two people, each with a child's best interests at heart, both feeling so intimidated they don't talk much with each other:

"I love working with children like Rosita. When it comes to working with family members, that's a different story. Rosita's father likes to hang around. He watches everything I do and makes me so nervous I can't think of anything to say to him," explains Tyresa, a toddler teacher.

"Having a child in child care is a new experience for me. I want to do it right for Rosita's sake, but I feel clumsy and unsure around her teacher, who seems to know it all. I don't even know what to say to her," says Juan, Rosita's father.

Teachers and family members sometimes don't talk because, like Tyresa and Juan, they are uncomfortable around each other. Sharing the care of a child can stir up normal and complex feelings such as guilt, jealousy, and competition that can get in the way. Teachers and family members may not speak the same language and need the help of a translator. Even when teachers and family members speak the same language, they often do not know what to say to one another. As a result, teachers and family members may find themselves at odds, dealing with grievances, real and imagined, that have a way of popping up when people don't talk together. The longer this goes on, the harder it is to begin a conversation.

The rest of this article offers ideas of topics that need discussing and examples of conversation starters. These are just suggestions that you can tailor to your situation. Get help from a translator when necessary. It's up to you, the infant care teacher, to get the conversation started — but once you do, let it become two-way communication.

Getting the Conversation Started: Helping Families Feel Welcome and Competent in Your Setting

Put yourself in a new family member's shoes for a moment:

You are leaving your child with someone you don't know very well in a strange place with lots of little chairs. You worry if you are doing the right thing. You don't know where to put your child's things or even if you should stand or sit, let alone what you should do if your child begins to cry. The thought of talking with a teacher floods you with memories of Mrs. Davis, whom everyone feared in the third grade. You feel guilty and sad and scared and fumbly, all the while hoping everything will turn out fine.

What could a teacher say that would help you feel welcomed?

What kinds of information do you need to feel competent in this new place?

Here are some examples of things caregivers might say to family members:

✣ "Hello, we are happy to see you. Welcome!"

✣ "Let me introduce you to _____ and _____, who are also teachers here."

✣ "Please sit down and join us."

✣ "Feel free to choose a puzzle or toy you think might interest your child."

✣ "Your child's supplies go here in this bin with her name on it."

✣ "Drawers and shelves are labeled so you can find whatever you need."

✣ "Help yourself — and your child — to a drink of milk or juice."

✣ "Let me know when you are getting ready to leave, and I'll come over and help you say goodbye to your child."

✣ "Let me know if you have a question or need a hand with anything."

Talking with Family Members About Your Partnership

"Working together as partners" sounds good, but how do you do it? Most parents don't know. It's up to you to lay a foundation that you both can then build on together.

Once again, slip on a pair of a family member's shoes:

What kinds of things do you think family members want and need to know about?

Here are some examples of questions family members in your program may wonder about, even if they don't ask you directly, and some sample answers that teachers might give to these questions:

✛ "When can we talk together?"

"We can talk each morning and at the end of the day when you come to pick up your child. But we also need other longer times to talk, without interruption. For this we have conferences and evening meetings. Of course, if one of us wants time to talk in between, let's agree we'll just say so and then arrange it."

✛ "What kinds of information do you need each day to take good care of my child?"

"When you tell me about your child's eating, toileting, sleeping, and play, you help me plan her day. If, for example, she didn't sleep much, I know she may be out of sorts and may need an early nap. I will give you this same information so you know what to expect when you take her home."

✛ "Will my child love you more than me?"

"You are your child's most important people. No one can take your place. Your relationship with your child is forever, over the years and across the miles. My role is to support both of you."

✛ "How can we help each other out day by day?"

"Labeling your child's clothes will help me keep track of them. Here's a marker you can use."

"Will you help me put the chairs up on the table so the floor can be cleaned tonight?"

"This morning your child was clinging to you when you said goodbye. I wasn't sure if you wanted me to take her out of your arms. What do you think we should do if that happens again?"

✛ "I have lots of questions. Is it all right to ask them?"

"Yes, please feel free to ask questions. No one has all the answers when it comes to infants and toddlers. Sharing our questions — then discovering answers together — is one of the ways we can work together to take care of your child."

✣ "What happens when we disagree?"

"Just as family members of the same child do when they disagree about things, we'll need to talk about our differences and decide together how we will handle them."

Reaping the Benefits

Like Tyresa and Juan, whom you met at the beginning, you and family members might be leaving a lot unsaid. Talking together is one of the most important things you can do to strengthen your partnership. The infants and toddlers you care for and about have everything to gain.

"When inclusion ... is fully embraced, we abandon the idea that children have to become 'normal' in order to contribute to the world. Instead, we search for and nourish the gifts that are inherent in all people. We begin to look beyond typical ways of becoming valued members of the community, and, in doing so, begin to realize the achievable goal of providing all children with an authentic sense of belonging."

     —Norman Kunc (1992)

Kunc's notion of fully embracing inclusion is critically important. Mindful of Kunc's notion, we draw on our expertise and experience in the fields of both early childhood care and education and early childhood special education to advocate for the perspective of children with disabilities or other special needs. Several approaches support this inclusive perspective:

✣ changing original language to represent children with different rates of growth and development;

✣ adding information to text that more clearly illustrates how a concept would also apply to children with disabilities or other special needs; and

✣ including examples that incorporate children with disabilities or other special needs, sometimes without making the disability the focus of the example.

The Individuals with Disabilities Education Act (IDEA) was initially signed three decades ago and the Americans with Disabilities Act (ADA) was passed in 1990. Yet we note that writers must still specify that "all children" means all children, *including children with disabilities or other special needs*. We have found that advocates of inclusive care need to continue

to make explicit the assumptions made in reference to "all" children. We wonder, therefore, what steps will help everyone naturally and consistently support and promote growth and development in all young children regardless of their individual or unique characteristics.

Two areas for consideration that we believe could more effectively promote an "authentic sense of belonging" are (1) rethinking professional preparation for early childhood and early childhood special education and early intervention, and (2) examining the existing structures or systems of accessing care for families of infants and toddlers. Through creating a dialogue around these issues, we hope to broaden professional perspectives of all who provide early care and education services.

Professional Preparation

For the most part, early childhood education (ECE) professionals and early intervention/early childhood special education (ECSE) specialists participate in professional preparation separately. Often ECE and ECSE programs at the college or university level are in separate departments, with classes generally taught by different instructors or professors, reinforcing the notion and practice that children with disabilities or other special needs belong in a separate educational category. We often see philosophical statements or curriculum guidelines about children in general without any reference to young children with disabilities or other special needs. In an integrated system, students of ECE and ECSE would study the same courses and work in the same laboratory programs, and teachers would enter the workforce more fully prepared for inclusive early care and education for all children.

When training encompasses young children who are typically developing as well as those with disabilities or other special needs, teachers feel prepared to serve all young children. Rather than feeling that working with children with disabilities or other special needs requires very specialized knowledge, they learn that training and experience in developmentally appropriate practice are exactly the foundation needed to work with ALL children. They learn that every child differs from the next, which means, for example, that children with Down syndrome differ from one another as much as they do from all other children. General information about Down syndrome becomes

meaningful when teachers come to know and understand the individual child with Down syndrome. The best information for getting to know and understand an individual child with disabilities or other special needs comes from forming partnerships with the family and specialists involved with that child.

Resources and courses that address forming these types of partnerships, ways to adapt routines and environments, and methods to document and communicate concerns regarding a child's development provide teachers with valuable tools for offering inclusive care and education. To serve young children with disabilities or other special needs in natural environments,[1] specialists in early intervention need a strong foundation in typical child development, familiarity with the elements of high-quality education and care for children from birth to age three, and techniques and a willingness to serve as a consultant rather than as a direct service provider.

---

1. As defined in the Individuals with Disabilities Education Act, a *natural environment* is a setting that is natural or normal for the child's age peers who have no disabilities and includes the home and community settings in which children without disabilities participate.

Increasingly, we see evidence that ECE and ECSE professionals are becoming more connected. They are relying on one another for expertise and accountability, not only because of recent legislation emphasizing that children should receive early intervention services and supports in their natural environments, but also because more families who require accessible and affordable child care believe that their children's needs can best be met in "regular" or general early care and education programs.

Systems of Supports and Services

Even when professionals in the ECE and ECSE fields work closely, they still operate in two separate systems while providing supports and services to families and children. Attitudes and assumptions about who needs care and who benefits from quality care continue to impact a family's access to services, supports, and child care. Everyone, therefore, should take greater responsibility participating in and promoting a dialogue of inclusion that makes explicit that "all" means every child. When children are valued for their individual strengths and needs, we will no longer need to qualify that ALL means

ALL. In the meantime, we must continue to advocate both for access to quality care and for options in supports and services for children regardless of their developmental needs.

We envision a system of care in which families can have access to early care and education as well as to intervention services — through the same seamless system rather than through separate systems. There are numerous community models of other types of services that link multiple systems, funding streams, program policies, and differentiated job roles to offer one-stop, simplified service delivery for families. As an example, in San Diego County there is a Center for Family Justice where a woman who has been battered can obtain in one location comprehensive services such as a restraining order, counseling for herself and her children, financial support, and medical attention. Professionals in the ECE and ECSE fields can learn from such successful community models to identify partners in joining forces to better serve families and children. In the end, this leads to shared philosophies of caregiving and professional cultures that support equal access and options for ALL families.

The tendency has been to assume that the *other* setting, the *other* teacher, the *other* program can best meet the learning and developmental needs of the infant and toddler with disabilities or other special needs. A key to successful inclusion is to move beyond these assumptions and to provide enrollment, services, supports, and access for families to include their children from the earliest opportunities in caregiving environments with their friends and same-age peers who are not at risk or who do not have disabilities.

By addressing the issues of professional preparation and by supporting innovative community approaches to child care, we can ensure the optimal growth and development for our very youngest children who have disabilities or other special needs. They will benefit from effective partnerships, creative problem solving, and provisions of adaptations in the caregiving environment when needed. In meeting these conditions of care, we will demonstrate through our actions that ALL means ALL and focus on providing "an authentic sense of belonging" for all children.

1 Infant Mental Health

By Jeree Pawl, Ph.D.

The phrase infant mental health is used in a number of ways, most often without any precise meaning. It always, however, speaks to the concern for the well-being and healthy development of all young children. It encompasses the wish to understand what best promotes and supports positive development and what interferes with it.

Many different kinds and sources of knowledge are involved in the effort to understand what the child needs to be as physically and emotionally healthy as she is able to be. Experts from a variety of fields study brain development, culture, relationships, language, socialization, moral development, temperament, and many other areas of relevance, and they have a great deal to say about what it is within the baby and outside of the baby that begins to influence his developmental paths.

There is also one additional expert. What would we call someone whose entire life has been devoted to the study of parents, other caregivers, the subtleties of interpersonal relationships, the regulation of feelings, the puzzling meaning of behavior, and the nature of conflict and cooperation? We would have to call this person a baby. That is what a baby does. He begins this effort immediately, and he never stops. It is his primary activity and it occurs within and around other major activities such as eating; being changed; kicking; making sounds; looking; recognizing the smells, touch, and sounds of the adults that care for him; and learning how to be with each one of them. Every child comes into the world especially designed to engage with those who care

for him. People are babies' very first and most compelling interest. They are captivated from the beginning. And we learn many of the most important things about babies by observing them.

Within this nest of earliest caretaking, the baby's experiences create her first senses of what this new world is like. These experiences join with her own unique potentials to create her world. For each baby it is a different world because each baby is different from every other baby. Timmy likes to be handled and rocked when he is upset, and Manda prefers her thumb and to be left alone. Wong Chen is happily content looking around him for long periods of time, but Eli gets quickly restless and needs a change of position or place. Arieta sleeps a lot. Arno sleeps barely at all. Not only do babies experience things differently, but they certainly have very different effects on those who care for them. Arieta's mother thinks it is fairly easy to care for a small baby, an "easy" baby. Arno's mother is exhausted and has a hard time telling day from night. Arno feels like a "difficult" baby.

People will figure out what their babies need quickly, slowly, or not at all. And there are situations in which those caring for a baby, for whatever reasons, have circumstances that seriously interfere with their paying attention to what their baby needs almost at all. People's values and beliefs about raising a child vary importantly, stemming from a particular culture, a blend of cultures, and their own unique life experiences.

Within their different worlds, babies watch, absorb, and learn how to manage their feelings, tell their feelings apart, express their feelings or not, and learn about the feelings of others. Within these profound connections with those who care for them, they may feel more or less safe, afraid, important, alone, or very pleased. They learn from these important people what they can expect, hope to expect, or never expect. Gradually, how they come to feel about themselves and about others is a central aspect of their well-being — their mental health. All people that children touch in significant ways affect these feelings and expectations. We observe children move; grow; creep; crawl; take turns making conversation; learn a word, a sign, a game; reach; and grasp in order to understand their physical and mental development. Intermingled with this, we also notice their comfort with themselves and oth-

ers and what their anxieties, worries, curiosities, and interests are. We notice also how they play and how they show pleasure and unhappiness, and we come to understand how they feel as well.

We do not expect every child to be like every other. They can be shy, feisty, demanding, stubborn, easygoing, solitary, or active. Those things we just need to notice, know, appreciate, and collaborate with. We begin to feel concerned when there is way too much of something or way too little.

Child care centers and family child care homes are very special places. They are not parking lots or even just safe places for a child to be when he is not in his home. They are unique unto themselves. Each is a whole community living space where the child continues to learn, absorb, and gather information. He learns not only from what is deliberately taught but from everything that happens with everyone in that space. Automatically, such environments make a positive or a negative contribution to the well-being, the mental health, and the overall development of children. Understanding this impact is crucial to shaping that result. In these places, there can be a coming together of parents, whose children are precious to them, with teachers, who strive to provide the care and experiences that the children and parents deserve. These teachers understand that they need to know the parents if they are to know and understand the child well enough. They know that the parents have an important role to play as collaborators. Parents, children, and teachers can create among them an atmosphere of exploration, self-expression, creativity, acceptance, respect, and a spirit of cooperation, good nature, and fun. This is a contribution to everyone's mental health, and everyone's mental health here is important.

When an infant care teacher understands the positive influence she can have on mental health, she will express this by

1. conveying awareness of a child's likes, dislikes, and ways of responding so the child feels seen, known, understood, and valued;

2. discovering with a child the meaning of his behavior;

3. acknowledging and accepting a child's expression of his feelings;

4. feeling free to delight and take pleasure in those unique interactions that occur only because of who both she and the child are;

5. joining in the child's pleasure in her accomplishments, even as the teacher notes the ways in which to support continued progress;

6. appreciating a child's uniqueness, strengths, and vulnerabilities, and liking what is special about him;

7. understanding a child's home context and including that world in his day in care;

8. supporting the child's family relationships and being aware of when a child misses or is anxious about a parent or other family member;

9. creating relationships with coworkers that allow a child to see and experience adults cooperating, collaborating, respecting, and trusting one another; and

10. implementing the structures of care (such as primary care and small group size) that support the ability of children and staff to form predictable, reliable, and meaningful relationships.

Infant mental health is many things. Its essence lies in the child's inner sense of well-being, which has many aspects and comes from many sources. Although infant mental health constitutes a field that is studied and thought about in many different areas of inquiry, it is not some mysterious thing up in the sky. Infant mental health is always living right in the room every single minute. Our interactions with and around infants have meaningful influences on them whether we are aware of it or not. The most important thing about it is to recognize and appreciate the continuous opportunities, such as those presented in the list above, to influence a child's well-being — his mental health. Knowing, caring

for, and spending a lot of time with very young children all have an influence on how they feel about themselves and others. Taking charge of that influence and reflecting on the impact of how we are interacting with a child is what is important. Realizing the opportunity to have the most positive effect we can is a remarkable privilege and one we certainly do not want to miss. Being concerned for the mental health infants and toddlers does not mean seeking a remedy for a problem. It is instead a proactive, positive goal — it means creating environments in which everyone can thrive.

Working with Traumatized Young Children in Child Care and Education Settings

By Alicia F. Lieberman, Ph.D.

Teachers and program leaders in child care programs often find themselves caring for young children who have had traumatic experiences. Information such as that presented here can be used to help young children function in a group care setting. Teachers may never learn about events that have led to a child's post-traumatic behaviors, and it is not a teacher's role to make any kind of diagnosis. Most of the behaviors described here occur within the typical range of behavior, yet with a child who has been traumatized, the behavior tends to be more extreme and intense. In these situations, the usual techniques and strategies that are generally successful with other children no longer work. Teachers and program leaders can learn about mental health resources in their community, possibly through the local child care resource and referral agency. Working closely with family members is an essential part of addressing issues that arise in the child care setting.

Exposure to traumatic events is a leading cause of death and injury in young children. For example, physical abuse and accidents are the leading cause of death in the first five years of life. Even when the child is not physically hurt, traumatic events can create serious and lasting emotional harm. Infants, toddlers, and preschoolers are particularly vulnerable because their capacity to protect themselves, understand what happened, and tolerate stress and fear is still immature.

Young children are completely dependent on adults for their physical safety and emotional well-being. Children can remember traumatic events starting in the first year of life and need the adult's help in coping with their fear. Unfortunately, caregivers are often unable to respond to the traumatized child's needs because they do not know what happened to the child or they believe that the child is too young to be affected by the traumatic event. When the special needs of traumatized children are not addressed, their behavior can disrupt the daily routine of the child care setting because their stress is often manifested in aggression, fearfulness, lack of compliance, and inability to learn. Even though caregivers may not ever know that children experienced trauma, their behaviors may indicate special needs. Addressing their needs involves understanding how young children respond to trauma and how child care providers can identify and care for traumatized children.

What Is Trauma?

A traumatic event happens when the child or another person is threatened with death or serious injury and the event is either experienced directly or witnessed by the child. All traumatic situations have an important element in common: The child is unable to control what is happening and is overwhelmed by fear, distress, or horror. Trauma always involves losing a feeling of safety. Witnessing a parent being attacked, injured, or killed is traumatizing even when the child is not physically hurt because the parent cannot be available as a source of protection.

Traumatic events can be inflicted intentionally (as in the case of physical abuse, domestic violence, and war), or they can happen accidentally (for example, in dog bites, near-drownings, and car accidents). Natural or man-made disasters can also be traumatic, as with earthquakes, hurricanes, floods, fires, and terrorist attacks. These events can occur as a single episode or as a series of episodes. Different traumatic circumstances often exist simultaneously. For example, child abuse is more frequent in families where there is domestic violence.

How Does Trauma Affect Young Children?

Traumatized children often show behaviors that seem out of control, fearful, disruptive, or excessively aggressive. The child's age and developmental level influence how the traumatic response is expressed. Preverbal children cannot describe what happened to them with words, but they show it through their behavior and play. Behaviors associated with trauma are described below.

1. Reliving the traumatic event. Children can be flooded by memories of terrifying events and behave as if the traumatic situation is happening again. For babies, reliving the traumatic event may be shown by inconsolable crying, motor dis-

organization, and bodily symptoms such as chronic vomiting and diarrhea without an organic reason. Other ways of showing reexperience of the trauma include the following:

a. *Post-traumatic play*. Young children often reenact aspects of the trauma in their play. For example, a physically abused child may play at hitting the doll for misbehaving, engaging in this behavior repeatedly and with high emotional intensity. Unlike typically adaptive play, which helps the child to express and master challenging experiences, posttraumatic play is rigid, repetitive, driven, lacks imagination (because it is a literal reenactment of the traumatic event), and fails to relieve anxiety.

b. *Preoccupation with the traumatic event*. The child constantly thinks about what happened and is easily distracted from other activities by the need to talk about it. For example, a two-year-old who witnessed his father battering his mother kept repeating "Mommy owie" in the course of the day while in child care, including during toileting and when put down for a nap.

c.   *Intense emotion, distress, or ag-gression at reminders of the trauma.* When children see or hear things that remind them of the traumatic event, they may respond with disorganized behavior and intense emotion. For example, a twelve-month-old who had recently received stitches on her cheek due to a dog bite screamed in panic whenever she saw a dog and whenever she saw a man wearing a white jacket, which reminded her of the doctor who performed the procedure. An eighteen-month-old started having intense and prolonged tantrums whenever his mother was out of his sight after being in a car accident where he was unhurt but his mother had to be hospitalized for three days for medical care.

d.   *Nightmares and dreams about the traumatic event.* Children might wake up screaming or describe a frightening dream. For example, a three-year-old who witnessed a knife fight woke up from a nap screaming, "No knife! No knife!"

2. Signs of agitation, restlessness, anxiety, and impulsivity. Traumatized children have difficulty relaxing. They often seem jumpy and nervous. They can overreact to loud noises, such as a siren, and they often get startled easily. They may have trouble falling asleep or staying asleep and can be hard to comfort, which can be frustrating for their caregivers. They may also have difficulty paying attention, concentrating on a task, and staying still. On the other hand, they may constantly be on the alert for signs of danger and become anxious and clingy when unpredictable changes in routine occur. Traumatized children can be wrongly diagnosed as hyperactive and treated with medication when professionals do not ask about the child's exposure to trauma or are not aware of how trauma can affect young children's behavior.

3. Aggressive or sexualized behavior and cruelty to animals. Children learn from what they see, and they imitate adult behavior because acting like the adults makes them feel competent and strong. Even when they have not witnessed or experienced violence, aggression in children is usually a sign that they feel frightened and insecure and they are trying to protect themselves by striking out first. A child who chronically behaves aggressively without noticeable cues from the situation (such as another child's grabbing a toy or pushing) may be behaving this way because of trauma. Sexualized behavior can be seen when children are attempting to relieve anxiety, when they have witnessed overstimulating adult behavior, or when they have been sexually abused. This sexualized behavior can take the form of children's excessive and intense rubbing of their private parts, most often with a worried facial expression. It can also take the form of aggressive curiosity in seeing other children's private parts, forcing other children to undress, or touching them without their consent. Typical sexual curiosity at this age is mutual, with the children showing interest rather than worry in the activity. Cruelty to animals is used by children as a discharge for their aggressive feelings when they do not have another safe way of venting. It involves hurting an animal repeatedly and on purpose, and it is different from a single episode of anger or accidentally hurting an animal. Traumatized children cannot control their aggression or sexualized behavior by themselves. They need understanding adults to help them gain control over their inappropriate behavior, reassure them that they are safe, and teach them socially appropriate ways of expressing their feelings. When guidance techniques do not help a child improve behavior, professional consultation is recommended. (An infant mental health consultation could be sought by the program leader, for example, or parents could be urged to pursue a psychological evaluation of the child.)

4. Multiple fears. When feeling unsafe, young children become fearful and have difficulty exploring their surroundings. Separation anxiety is the most frequent of these fears. Children who are afraid of being left become clingy, particularly during transitions or in new situations. Fear of the dark and fear of monsters are also common. All young children show some fears as a typical part of development, but the fears of traumatized children are more numerous and intense. These fears should always be taken seriously because they are real for the child, even when they seem imaginary to the adult. Infants, toddlers, and preschoolers need to be reassured that the adult will take care of them and keep them safe. Helping family members to reassure the child is also important because it builds a bridge between the child care setting and the home that increases the child's sense of trust in the caregivers.

5. Losing developmental gains.

Following a traumatic event, children can regress in their behavior. For example, an older toddler may revert to baby talk or relapse in toilet training. Children may also withdraw from social interaction and stop showing joy, spontaneity, pleasure in learning, and interest in exploration. In general, it is important to remember that all children have a "bad day" occasionally and that the behaviors described above are shown at one time or another by most children, particularly at times of transition. These behaviors should become a cause of concern about the possibility of trauma only when they are repeated over several weeks and when they interfere with the child's social relationships, ability to explore, readiness to learn, and other important aspects of development.

How Can the Child Care Provider Help?

When they are aware of children's developmental needs, child care providers can help children learn to cope with their traumatic responses. Programs can increase caregivers' awareness by providing ongoing professional development on caring for children who have experienced trauma. The following ten practices are useful in providing the child with a sense of safety and include involving the child's family members whenever possible as partners in the effort to help the child. Although most of these suggestions are helpful when caring for any child, including children who have experienced trauma, the last three are especially important for supporting the traumatized child in particular.

1. Provide a safe environment with predictable daily routines.

2. Ensure stable relationships with caregivers and teachers.

3. Understand that difficult child behaviors, including aggression, noncompliance, and impulsivity, are often triggered by situations that remind the child of a traumatic event or are the result of chronic stress or maltreatment.

4. Help the child with separation anxiety by providing reassurance that the parents will return at the end of the day and by providing consistent reassurance about other fears.

5. Avoid disciplinary methods that might frighten an already traumatized child, including losing control, raising one's voice, harsh language, angry reactions, and isolation.

6. Work collaboratively with the family members on a course of action to reassure and support the child.

7. Use play, exercise and body movement, music, books, and other activities to help the child cope with intense negative feelings.

8. Whenever possible, obtain information from the family members about the traumatic event to understand how the child is being affected.

9. Consult with an infant mental health professional (in collaboration with the child's family members), when possible, about child behaviors that may indicate exposure to trauma in order to discuss behavioral strategies that might help the child.

10. Recommend to the child's family members that the child be evaluated by an infant mental health program or professional when the child's behavior is chronic, severe, and does not respond to the interventions described above.

Environments for Infants and Toddlers

By Louis Torelli, M.S.Ed.

The physical environment has a powerful impact on children's learning and development. Well-designed environments support exploration, give young children a sense of control, and enable children to engage in focused, self-directed play. The physical environment also affects relationships. Well-designed spaces evoke a sense of security by offering intimate play areas within the larger environment that allow children to explore and reflect while still being connected to their caregiver and the rest of the group. This sense of security is a prerequisite in the formation of a healthy sense of self, or identity. In appropriately designed classrooms, children are given an opportunity to play independently and in small groups as they choose, and teachers are supported in their role as observers and facilitators of children's learning and development.

Developing a Vision: Creating a Master Plan

Whether developing a new child care facility, remodeling an existing center, or attempting a makeover of a classroom or family child care home, planning is the key to a successful design. A well-thought-out plan will help to avoid wasting time and money on short-term, temporary fixes that may need to be addressed later. It is wiser to make changes in stages than to compromise quality by trying to take on too much at once. Start by identifying the improvements desired.

If major changes are planned, enlist a design professional to help optimize use of space and budget and insure that the renovation complies with all code requirements. Identify all resources, not only available funds. Parents or other family members may be able to assist in carpentry, plumbing, and landscaping. They may also be able to help in soliciting donations from businesses. Stores in the local community may be able to donate lumber and carpeting.

Key Criteria for Creating Quality Environments

While environments for care differ widely, there are certain elements that contribute to a quality experience for infants and toddlers.

Group Size. The number of children cared for in one classroom affects infants' health and well-being. With larger groups there is an increase in upper respiratory illnesses and ear infections (Bartlett and others, 1986; Bell and others, 1989). In crowded spaces there is more conflict, aggressiveness, and unfocused play (Ruopp and others, 1979). Infants should be cared for in groups of no more than six to eight children; toddlers, in groups of no more than eight to twelve children.

Room Size. The size of each classroom must be large enough to meet individual children's needs and the group's needs. Provide a *minimum* of 50 square feet of usable space per child. If, however, the current setting provides a smaller classroom with a larger group size, it is critical to view everything that is available as a potential learning environment. For example, a teacher might take three or four young toddlers into the hallway with push and pull toys, balls, or ride-on toys. Or, teachers can organize daily schedules in a way that allows for smaller groups to use the same space at different times during the day. For instance, one teacher might be outside with a few children while another teacher is inside with the other children.

Sinks and Toilets. The right number of appropriately placed plumbing fixtures is a necessary requirement of a well-designed classroom. Food preparation and diapering areas should be separate and allow for full supervision of the room. Child-sized hand-washing sinks should be located in every classroom at the right height for the age group served, as should appropriately sized toilets when serving older toddlers.

Sculpting the Environment. An infant and toddler environment must accommodate a variety of activity areas, such as eating, messy play, reading, manipulative play, and symbolic play, as well as diapering and napping. The classroom must also be flexible enough to support children's varying developmental abilities, including children's special needs.

Through the use of items such as platforms, lofts, recessed areas, low walls, fabric canopies, risers, wall storage, and toy shelves placed along the periphery of the classroom, the room can be sculpted

to provide a variety of age-appropriate activities. Couches, chairs, and tables can be used (particularly in family child care homes) to assist in defining the play space. Placing activity areas along the walls of the room will help to create boundaries that support individual and small-group play as well as provide teachers with the ability to closely supervise the entire group.

The placement of each activity area is as important as the specific furnishings and materials in those areas. A well-thought-out space plan can actually make a classroom or home feel and function as one 25 to 30 percent larger than one with a poorly laid-out plan. The importance of an optimal space plan becomes even more compelling when working in a smaller room or one with a larger group size.

Classroom Furnishings. To complement furnishings such as high-quality wooden commercial furniture, infant and toddler programs should also turn to home and import stores to "cozy up" the room. Some examples of good items to consider are washable quilts and pillow shams, upholstered chairs (with washable slipcovers), cloth hammocks, gliders, armoires for additional storage, fabric to create canopied areas, and woven baskets to display balls, dolls, and other play items. A track light or wall-mounted lamp can help to distinguish the reading area from other activity spaces. Plants and a fish tank can help bring nature indoors. Of course, children's health and safety must always be considered first when choosing materials and equipment. Keep in mind that all materials and surfaces must be washable, lighting cords must be out of children's reach, and plants must be nontoxic.

Outdoor Play Area. Whenever possible, every classroom and family child care home should provide direct access to the outside play space. The outside play area should be an extension of the classroom. An appropriately designed outdoor play area should include many natural elements, such as grass, gentle hills, sand, dirt, tree stumps, shade trees, and water sources. It should feel more like a park than a playground. Benches, trellises, planter boxes, hammocks, and wind chimes are some of the possibilities. With a thoughtful design, the natural landscape will itself provide opportunities for gross motor play. Every indoor activity has the potential of having an outdoor counterpart. Outdoor counterparts can also help to compensate for indoor environments with less-than-optimal square footage.

Reflective Practice

By Claire Lerner, L.C.S.W.

What Is Reflective Practice? Reflective practice is the process of continuous learning through thoughtful examination of one's work. Donald Schön (1983) described three key components of reflective practice: *reflection for action* (planning ahead) and *reflection on action* (thinking back on what happened) in order to enhance capacity for effective *reflection in action* (thinking in the moment, which is perhaps the most difficult). Using a reflective approach is especially important for teachers of infants and toddlers because of the intensely emotional and critical nature of their work — promoting the healthy development of young children. The more charged a situation, the more likely it is that one will be reactive (acting before thinking), which when working with young children and families can lead to unintended, negative consequences.

What Reflective Practice Looks Like

Louisa arrives early one day, during lunch-time, to pick up her two-year-old son, Marco. Marco's teacher, Trish, notices that Louisa looks distressed. Louisa pulls Trish aside and angrily tells her that she had no idea the kids fed themselves and that she wants Marco fed directly by Trish.

Trish is shocked and quite angry her-self. She believes two-year-olds should feed themselves and is beside herself that Louisa expects Trish to give Marco that kind of attention with seven other toddlers to supervise. Trish realizes that she is too angry to respond effectively to Louisa right now. She needs time to think this through. She tells Louisa that she is sorry Louisa is so unhappy and that they clearly need to discuss this further. Louisa agrees to come early the next day to al-low them time to meet. After Louisa and Marco leave, Trish returns to the lunch table and her colleague, Jenna, leans over and gives Trish a warm squeeze.

During naptime, Trish tells Jenna what happened. Jenna shares Trish's surprise at Louisa's reaction and suggests she talk to the center director, Christi. Christi makes time to meet with Trish later in the day. When Trish recounts the incident to her,

Christi empathizes with how surprised and dismayed Trish must have felt and gives her credit for taking the time to think things over and not reacting. Christi asks about Trish's own thoughts about feeding toddlers. To help Trish think about it from different perspectives, they brain-storm together possible reasons why Lou-isa would not want Marco to feed himself even though he is clearly able to do so. At the end of their meeting, Christi suggests Trish ask Louisa why she wants Marco fed by an adult and then for Trish to share her own philosophy about independent feed-ing and see if they can negotiate a solu-tion. Christi offers to watch Trish's group while she meets with Louisa.

When they meet, Louisa tells Trish that in her family young children are fed because it is part of the caretaking ritual — it is a way children are shown love. While she knows Marco will eventually feed himself, right now she does not expect or want him to do this. Louisa also mentions that her family has been "on her back" about how skinny Marco is. She wants an adult to feed him to make sure he eats enough.

Trish tells Louisa how helpful it is to understand "where she is coming from" (and thinks to herself, "That was something we really missed when we met the family and asked about their beliefs and values!"). Trish then shares with Louisa why the children feed themselves at the center — because the adult-child ratio precludes one-to-one feeding of toddlers and because self-care skills are taught and valued. Trish acknowledges the conflict between the center's and the family's philosophies. She also validates Louisa's concern about Marco's food intake. Trish mentions that she has, in fact, noticed that Marco has been eating less, but she had assumed it was just a stage. They agree that it's time to consult Marco's pediatrician. Trish offers to sit next to Marco at lunchtime and to feed him when she can, but she explains why she doesn't feel comfortable forcing him to eat. If it turns out that his intake is a problem, they will consult with a nutritionist to develop a plan they both can implement. Louisa thanks Trish for her time and apologizes for getting so angry the day before.

Imagine how things might have turned out had Trish not used reflection as a key tool in her work. She could have reacted angrily, making Louisa feel discounted and even angrier than she was. Had Trish not been open to hearing about Louisa's thoughts and feelings, Louisa might have been much less willing to consider Trish's point of view, making negotiation and working together to develop a good solution for Marco almost impossible. Finally, consider the negative impact on Marco of ongoing conflict between his mother and teacher, or of Louisa's pulling Marco from the program altogether, if the center would not care for him according to the family's beliefs and values.

What It Takes

You can see from this vignette that implementing reflective practice requires that a child care setting have

1. An administration that values reflection as an essential tool for providing quality care and one that creates a structure that encourages the development of staff relationships based upon mutual respect, collaboration, consistency, and safety. Such relationships support reflective practice.

2. Reflective supervision — a model of supervision that provides a safe place for teachers to *look at and listen* to themselves in relationship to their work, to acknowledge and wonder

about their own feelings and reactions, and to carefully observe what families and children are telling and showing them. Importantly, it allows teachers to *learn* from the situation — putting together what they understand about their own reactions and what they understand about the child and family to develop a sensitive and effective response.

3. Teachers who are a resource to one another for support and learning.

Ways to Incorporate Reflective Practice into Child Care Settings

✛ Make time at staff meetings for teachers to bring up challenges and for supervisors to facilitate a reflective approach to problem solving so staff members can learn together.

✛ Make time for reflective supervision. Reflective supervision can be done one to one or in small groups. Ideally, it occurs weekly. When starting out, it might work best to provide monthly opportunities. It is most effective when it is regular and uninterrupted.

✛ Provide flexibility so that teachers have adequate time for meaningful discussions with families.

Every Child Is a Cultural Being

By Carol Brunson Day, Ph.D.

In order to make genuine progress to address human diversity in early education, we need strategies that go deeper than approaches that stem from our desire to "respect" cultural differences. Beyond learning to reserve judgment about different cultural practices, we need to question the tendency to think about white children of the European-based dominant culture as exhibiting *ordinary human behaviors* while thinking about children of other ethnic ancestries as exhibiting *cultural behaviors*.

To do this, we must fundamentally avoid having one value system serve as the standard against which behavior is judged or measured. Instead, we would see the dominant worldview as one among many. In reality, all children are cultural beings. Their beliefs, values, and behavior stem from rich cultural perspectives that are rooted in early experiences with their families and communities.

Shifting perspective in this way opens many possibilities for transforming our knowledge about how children develop and for enhancing what we can do to help them. Working diligently together at the program level, families, teachers, and other staff members can make great strides by engaging in actions such as the following:

❖ Read what has been written about the development of children and families by researchers and theorists from a wide variety of cultural backgrounds.

❖ Remain open to adding to the training library material from diverse sources about developing children.

❖ Search for cultural bias in the theories and practice to which one has traditionally subscribed.

❖ Be reflective about bias in one's own thinking and become articulate about the cultural lens through which one views the world.

❖ Expand one's horizons to understand different cultural perspectives and appreciate that one's own cultural perspective is one among many.

❖ Create a safe climate for raising difficult issues and dealing with them openly and honestly.

❖ Develop strategies to prevent biases from being obstacles to children's development.

❖ Create an environment where home culture is integrated into the program as an important developmental goal for children and families.

❖ Explore ways to be receptive and responsive to different cultural perspectives while maintaining shared values.

❖ Uncover cultural and ethnic bias in the program and in the surrounding community.

As early education programs strive to promote development for all children, those from diverse cultures as well as those in the mainstream, meeting the challenge of making everyone's culture visible will do more than merely improve program practice — it will reshape the entire field. To discover ways to educate all children, we must also consider the unique differences of individuals. An important influence on these differences is one's culture. As our understanding of culture's influence on the development of all people deepens, our understanding of human universals will increase. So as we work to discover the developing cultural child, we at the same time unveil the human child.

Socialization and Guidance with Infants and Toddlers

By Janis Keyser, M.A.

"Mine!" "No-o-o-o!" "Wha-a-a-!" What do they want?

When we understand the reasons for infant and toddler behavior, we can respond to it in ways that support children's healthy growth and development and simultaneously decrease our worry and frustration. Infants and toddlers are working hard to understand their new feelings and ideas, to figure out their worlds, and to learn *how* to interact with other children and adults.

Most infant and toddler behavior that is difficult for adults is part of healthy development. A crying baby is using the best tool she has to communicate her needs to her caregiver. An older infant who is mad because an adult took the pen away from him is demonstrating that he now remembers what he is interested in and won't be easily distracted with another unrelated toy. A toddler who bites another child might be trying to figure out how to express her frustration or checking out her friend's feelings.

Here are some assumptions underlying effective socialization and guidance:

- Every interaction with a child is an opportunity to teach something; and every time we interact with a child, we are teaching something, whether we realize it or not — even during conflict or difficult interactions.

- The purpose of guidance is to help children learn about themselves and to teach them successful ways to interact with others. The purpose is never to punish, scare, or hurt a child.

- Behind every behavior is a healthy impulse. Even if the behavior itself is hurtful, it still makes sense from the child's perspective and demon-

strates some underlying competence. The child may be trying to express an idea or a feeling, ask a question, test a hypothesis, or connect with another person. From the child's perspective, his behavior is the best way he knows to get his needs met or communicate his message.

- If we can figure out the child's perspective or point of view, we can help her learn positive, safe, and successful behaviors to express herself and get her needs met.

Here are some actions to consider when helping children learn:

Look for the reason for the behavior you want to change. Observe when it happens, talk to coworkers and parents, and think about child development. Ask yourself, "What is it this child is trying to accomplish?"

Let the child know you want to understand what she is trying to express or figure out. "It looks like you are interested in how that pen works." "I hear you crying. I'm listening so I can understand you." "It looks like you both really want that truck."

Provide information to the child. "I can't let you play with this pen, because it has a sharp end that could poke you." "The water in the toilet isn't clean to play with." "When you hit him, it hurts." Even if the child can't fully understand the information you give him, he feels respected when you explain the reason to him.

Give the child a positive limit. Tell the child what you want her to do, instead of what you don't want her to do. "Give me the pen," rather than, "Don't play with the pen." Children don't usually hear the "don't" at the beginning of sentences.

Suggest another way for the child to express himself. Instead of distracting, "Come over here and we'll do a puppet show," suggest an alternative for the child to express his idea or do his research. "You look so interested in splashing. The toilet isn't a safe place for you to play, but here's a tub of water for you to splash in." The child is not only more likely to cooperate, but he also gets a chance to feel good about his idea.

Offer the child a choice. Toddlers need practice making their own decisions. We can give them that practice by setting up two good choices from which they can pick. "It's time to change your diaper. Do you want me to carry you, or do you want to walk over?"

Ensure safety. *Always* tell children what you are doing when you move them or touch them. "I'm going to pick you up and take you back to the play area." "I'm going to stop your hand from hitting Niko." With infants and toddlers, we often need to intervene physically to help them move or stop their bodies. It is essential that we do this in a loving, clear, and informative manner.

Follow through and anticipate. Older infants and toddlers are good at remem-

Positive limits...	Rather than negative
Keep your feet on the floor. Climb on the stairs.	*Don't climb on the table.*
Food stays on the table.	*Don't throw your food.*
Be gentle with your friend. "Ask her to 'Move.'"	*Don't hit her.*
You can ask him for a turn with the toy.	*Don't grab toys.*

bering what they were doing. They will often go right back to the activity you just stopped. Observe, stay close, and help them redirect their ideas in a safe way, again (and again) if necessary.

Model the behavior you want children to learn. Your tone, body, and voice convey as much meaning as your words. Strive to be clear, firm, loving, understanding, serious, calm, optimistic, but never punitive. Your gentle touch with children lets them know you respect them and provides a model for how they can touch their friends.

Avoid punishment, shame, fear, or belittling. These undermine the trust and self-confidence children need to learn positive self-control. When children are punished, they learn to fear the person they are supposed to trust the most. Effective socialization and guidance require the trust, comfort, and confidence that come from a supportive, nurturing relationship.

Beyond Baby Talk: Speaking with Babies

By Dolores G. Norton, Ph.D.

Eleven-week-old Gus is lying in his stroller, being pushed back and forth by his grandmother. He is waiting for his mother to come out of a meeting to nurse him. I turn from speaking to his grandmother and begin to bend over his stroller. As I bend closer, his eyes fasten on my face and widen, alert with expectant curiosity. With my own eyes widening, bending even closer, I speak directly to him. I use the elongated, soft-pitched, well-defined syllables used by most societies to speak with their babies, which we recognize as child-directed language. Focusing on my eyes, and then my lips, he listens intently. Arms at the ready, one leg jiggling, his lips moving, he struggles to get out a sound to talk back to me. When the sound comes, a soft short "A-ahhh," he is so pleased that both legs kick furiously. With eyes still glued to my face, he makes another sound, more distinct than the first. Delighted, I coo back, coming in closer, watching carefully to learn what sounds or words catch his interest. He makes more sounds. I mimic his sounds and add new ones. "A-ahhh, what did Gus say?" "A-ahhh, tell me about it." By this time his little arms and legs are pumping vigorously. He is smiling. I am smiling. We are both lost in the mutual joy of human interaction and communication.

Babies are learning from the moment of birth. As early as three days old, they intensively absorb everything around them as they attempt to make sense of their new world. Their favorite sources from which to gather this information are an animated human face and its voice. Communicating with language with babies is far more than just engaging in baby talk. We know now that speaking with babies influences brain development, rapidity of language development, understanding of the world around them, and their ability to learn.

There is a growing body of neuroscience research showing that early speaking with babies actually increases the formation and connections of neural pathways in the brain. These connections between neural pathways contribute to children's later capacity to control emotions and behavior, to relate to others, and to learn. Toddlers whose parents talk more with them have larger vocabularies than children whose parents speak with them less. Researchers at the University of Chicago found that by age two, children of mothers who talked to them more knew 295 more words than children of less talkative mothers (Huttenlocher, 1984).

Daily routines provide a fertile time to talk with babies. When we describe to them what we are doing in our regular routines of diapering, feeding, bathing, or playing, we help them to order their world and to feel more secure. We also send strong signals that stimulate the growth of synapses in the brain and biochemical changes that support cognitive development.

✤ Children begin to *learn the names of the objects* in the environment through the adult's labeling ("See the juice.").

✤ They begin to *understand their relationships* to objects and people ("It's orange juice." "Now Mommy pours the juice.").

- They *develop a sense of self and control* that soothes and leads to being comfortable in their environment ("First, we put on your socks, then your shoes.").

- They *sharpen their sensory knowledge* ("The water is warm." "Splash the water." "Let's taste the cereal." "Is it good?").

- They *learn to ponder questions* ("What is that?" "Is it a cat? "What does the cat say?").

- They *develop their imagination,* ("Let's pretend." "The cat says, 'Meow!'").

Since good teachers impart information, ask questions, and stir up children's imaginations, Jerome Bruner, cognitive psychologist at Harvard University, calls this type of talk *the language of education* used in the schools (1986). For instance, children can become familiar with naming and describing objects, feelings, and ideas through conversations with teachers. Use of such talk with babies and toddlers can give them familiarity with what they will encounter in prekindergarten.

Note that we are using the phrase "speaking *with*" instead of "speaking *to*" babies. This is to remind us that learning takes place best in the context of warm, interactive relationships that tell children they are heard and enjoyed and that we are listening and communicating. Thus, they intuit that they are important little persons. Speaking with babies should be interactive. Non-interactive, flat, one-dimensional speaking (such as on television) is not effective with babies and toddlers. The give-and-take of engaged physical, verbal, and sensory interactions that babies experience with others become keys to further their brain, language, social–emotional, and cognitive development. This occurs when the teacher and the children tap routinely into the mutual joy of interaction and communication that little Gus and I shared for those few moments.

The heart of early learning for infants and toddlers is nurtured by their first relationships with adults. Early reading for older infants (ages 8 to 18 months) and toddlers (ages 16 to 36 months) is about human interaction and creating interest in books and stories. This concept paper offers a practical guide for facilitating responsive book reading with very young children through adult-child relationships. The following information reminds us that reading *is* a social-emotional experience that is delicately influenced and organized by the emotions of children as well as adults.

pace, and (4) sensory exploration.

The Role of the Adult

The introduction of early book reading for infants and toddlers begins with the adult. The role of the adult in a child's life is pivotal to the child's learning experiences. Children are dependent upon adults for survival, security, care, and understanding of how the world works around them. It is through these early experiences with the adults that care and know about them that children come to learn about literacy.

The most inspiring ways adults may facilitate book reading with very young children are set in motion in a number of ways, including the following:

✢ Asking what kinds of books and/or reading experiences appeal to very young children. Consider the use of colors and textures. This approach can

✢ Having books available and easily accessible in the environment and during caregiving routines such as diaper changing and nap time;

✢ Providing consistent opportunities (both spontaneous and intentional) to engage children in book reading;

✢ Honoring the uniqueness of the child's contribution to reading by expanding on the child's cues and personal ways of communicating;

✢ Personalizing the stories to extend children's awareness of themselves and their environment;

✢ Including culturally and ethnically diverse books, some of which are representative of the languages of the children's families;

✢ Using your voice to bring the characters shown in the book to life — voice inflection often draws children deeper into a story;

- Modeling for children your joy of reading through singing, laughing, talking, and playing with the words in a book — your emotions influence their interest in the beginning processes of reading; and

- Repeating and reviewing with children what the story was about helps strengthen their comprehension.

Reading Together

In Jasmine's toddler classroom, which is delightfully named the Dinosaur Room, three toddlers are asleep, and Spencer, age 22 months, has just awakened from a nap. Jasmine is sitting on the floor. Spencer has just climbed into her lap and nestled in. He takes a little while to wake up, and Jasmine knows this — they often read books together when he awakens before the other children. It is a time they both look forward to and enjoy. Jasmine takes two books she knows Spencer likes from the shelf, one with a bear on the front and one with a duck on the front. She holds both books in front of Spencer and asks, "Which book should we read... the duck book or the one with the bear?" She waits quietly to watch his cues. Spencer looks at the bear book and begins to reach for it. Jasmine acknowledges Spencer's response by handing him the book and saying, "It looks like you want to read the book about the bear." As he opens the book, she asks Spencer, "What do you see?" before she reads the actual page. Spencer opens it to the middle and finds the page he is looking for where there is a red bird. Jasmine says, "Ah, you found the red bird again, and what do you think that bird is doing?" "Eat worms, yuck," says Spencer. Jasmine laughs, "I wonder what worms taste like." Spencer cranes his neck to look at her. "Worms," he says matter of factly. They look at the page and continue their discussion until Spencer turns to another page.

Sharing Space

Sharing space is a two-way experience between children and adults. This involves an atmosphere of trust. Close proximity allows for an exchange of nonverbal messages and supports emotional connectedness with children. Holding children close either on your lap, chest, or simply side-by-side reminds children of your presence and emotional availability.

Awareness of Pace

When reading through a book, move at a pace that feels comfortable for children. Be thoughtful as you take a slow and steady pace to engage them fully in book reading. Infants and toddlers will typically let you know what works and does not work for them through their vocalizations, facial and body expressions, and the handling of a book (e.g., cooing, babbling, turning away, arching their backs, or turning the pages rapidly).

Awareness of children's pace also includes careful consideration of your voice. Think about how you use your voice to monitor and regulate the messages you send while reading with a child. A respectful, calm, and comforting voice can reinforce for children that "there is no place I would rather be right now." The emphasis is on the experience of being together with infants and toddlers when reading rather than reading without the children's emotional engagement.

Sensory Exploration

Reading is a multisensory experience for infants and toddlers and includes interactive participation. Children's minds grow when they are able to play with and explore a variety of materials and the living things around them. Children can offer you wonderful information about who they are through the ways in which they explore materials. Note how children use all of their senses, such as "mouthing" or using their hands to open and close a book repeatedly. Let your observations and discoveries of children guide you in finding the most meaningful and safe ways to create responsive reading experiences, thereby allowing them to show their natural passion to actively learn.

Endless Learning Possibilities

Book reading with infants and toddlers is a natural and inspiring way to promote growth and development. An interactive approach to reading creates wonderful memories for young children. Books have a powerful way of influencing children's connections to their immediate world. When young children experience responsive reading, they look forward to opportunities to be read to and to "read."

Respectful Teaching with Infants and Toddlers

By Mary Jane Maguire Fong, M.S.

At birth, infants begin an amazing journey. Fueled with curiosity and supported by their families, infants set out to explore the world around them. Within months, many infants enter an infant program and find their base of support expanded to include infant care teachers. How does an infant care teacher support the curious infant? What does it mean to teach infants? When viewed from the perspective of guiding active and curious infants in their discovery of the world around them, the idea of teaching is seen as being respectful of who the child is and what the child naturally does. Respectful teaching is defined as providing care and education that is attuned to the individual and developmental needs, abilities, and interests of the children in the group. Respectful teaching is directly related to what children actually do as they explore and discover.

What does respectful teaching look like with infants and toddlers? Interestingly, the same ingredient that fuels infant learning fuels infant teaching: curiosity. Curious infants do best when matched with curious adults who are just as intent in their desire to learn about the infants in their care as the infants are to learn about the world before them. Guiding infant learning begins and ends with sensitive observation and requires a blend of respectful curiosity, thoughtful reflection, and flexible planning.

Observing and Noting

Curious teachers begin their work by watching, listening, and carefully thinking about that which they see and hear. As they greet and spend time with each family in their program, teachers listen for beliefs, values, expectations, and life experiences that make each infant and each family unique. Teachers also get to know the infants in their care by observing how they approach people and spaces before them. By watching and listening, teachers find out what, with whom, and how infants play. All of this information provides clues as to what infants are working on developmentally.

In all these ways curious teachers gather valuable information about the infants in their care. They compare what they observe to the rich body of child development research on how young children develop their bodies, their minds, their social strategies, and their personalities. Doing so helps them make thoughtful decisions in planning for infants' learning.

How do teachers turn their observations and reflections into useful written plans? Teachers begin with simple notes — brief, clear descriptions of key aspects they wish to remember. These observational notes of children's play and interactions form the foundation for infant curriculum. A teacher might make the following note after watching several of her toddlers play in a small trickle of water they discover in the yard.

Joan's Observation, May 5: *For about twenty minutes, Mario and Taeko repeatedly dropped twigs into a stream of water running through the dirt from the lawn outside the fence. They giggled and shouted with joy as they ran back and forth, following the twigs floating downstream.*

Reflecting and Discussing

Such a moment of play engages not only the curious mind of the child but also the curious mind of the teacher. Together with colleagues and infants' families, teachers think, talk, and wonder about observational notes. Doing so with others helps teachers clarify and expand their thinking about what infants are learning. This leads naturally to pondering, "How might we support what the infants are doing?" or "How might we add an interesting challenge by adding novelty, surprise, or complexity?" With one serving as notetaker, teachers come up with ideas and make a list or a web diagram, formed by writing the observed interest or issue in the center and writing ideas from the discussion on lines extending out from the center (see example below). The intent is to freely brainstorm all options for supporting the play or issue and to record all possibilities before deciding on a plan.

From the observation of children's play in the trickle of water, teachers might generate the following possibilities.

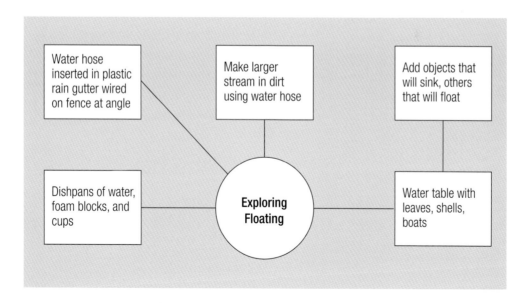

As teachers discuss the possibilities, they consider, "Is the toddlers' play focused on dropping objects into the flowing water and watching the current carry them along, or is it focused on finding things that float?" Through their discussion, they agree that the play is more focused on "flowing water." They decide to offer more experimentation with flowing water by introducing the plastic rain gutter wired to the fence, a new play encounter that will provide a similar but slightly more challenging experience.

Planning and Implementing

Once teachers decide on an idea, they prepare a brief, written plan to organize their work and make it visible to others. A useful plan describes what will be done, why, and what preparations need to be made. The plan to create an encounter with floating objects in a current of water might look something like the Observation and Plan on page 121.

Observing and Reflecting

Directly on the plan, teachers note what infants actually do in response to the plan, briefly recording observations they want to remember for later use. Such notes help teachers identify and describe infants' development and learning. What emerges is a study document that teachers can use in several ways. The observational notes provide evidence of infants' development and learning, key information to share with both families and program administrators. The observational notes also help teachers generate new possibilities for subsequent curriculum.

Observation and Plan

Observation: Idea that prompts this plan

M & T delighted in floating twigs in a stream of water running through the dirt.

Plan: May 10, teacher Joan and four toddlers

Wire to the fence, at an angle, a water trough made from plastic rain gutter. Insert a water hose turned on low. Below lower end, place tub, foam pieces, boats, leaves, seed pods, flowers, and other floatable items.

Observation and Reflection

Observation: What children do in response to plan

M drops a boat into the trough and watches as it floats down to tub. C throws items into tub, laughing when she makes a splash. T watches M's boat float down the trough, picks it up from tub and repeats M's actions. M & T continue dropping items at upper end of trough and run to retrieve them at bottom. M notices hose, pulls it out, and looks through open end of trough. Water flow stops, but C continues splashing toys and doesn't notice. T stares at empty trough but doesn't look to upper end, fills cup in tub, and dumps it into trough at midpoint. M puts hose back in the trough, looks at flowing water, removes hose for a second, and then replaces it in trough.

Reflection

It appears that M discovered the cause-and-effect relationship between the hose and the running water. T used a cup as a tool to put water back into the trough. Much cooperation and seemingly effortless sharing of close space and materials! Maybe next we'll put rain gutter and same materials on slanted ground.

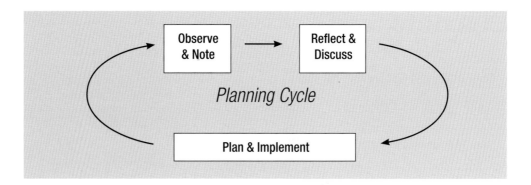

Planning Cycle

What emerges is a planning cycle — beginning with observation, which prompts reflection, which leads to planning, then implementation, which generates observation, which again leads to reflection and implementation.

The planning cycle is flexible. It guides play encounters that take place over a period of weeks, such as a teacher's creating possibilities for children to explore moving water. Or it guides a teacher's work in one afternoon of play. For example, a teacher who sees several infants climb onto a low shelf can rearrange the furniture in the play space to create more opportunities for climbing and observe and note what they do in response. The planning cycle also helps teachers plan for individual children. For example, teachers can use the planning cycle to organize their thinking and strategies for working with a child who shows a pattern of taking toys from other children.

The most compelling feature of the reflective planning cycle is that it makes teaching fun and rich with adventure for both children and adults. As a guide for teaching infants, the planning cycle takes participants on a delightful journey of discovering how infants explore the intriguing world before them. Within the process of the reflective planning cycle, infants and toddlers have the time and opportunity to pursue their interests, develop their cognitive skills, and think creatively. Infant care teachers also have the opportunity to engage in a discovery process. As children explore and discover the world, the teacher explores and discovers with the children. Seen through the children's eyes, the world the teacher shares with them becomes a more fascinating and dynamic place.

References

Baker, C. 2000. The Care and Education of Young Bilinguals: An Introduction for Professionals. Clevedon, UK: Multilingual Matters.

Baron-Cohen, S. Y.; and R. Staunton. 1994. "Do Children with Autism Acquire the Phonology of Their Peers? An Examination of Group Identification Through the Window of Bilingualism," First Language, 14 (42, Part 3), 241-248.

Bartlett, A.V.; P. Orton; and M. Turner. 1986. "Day Care Home: The Silent Majority of Child Day Care," Review of Infectious Disease, 8, 663–668.

Bell, D.M.; D.W. Gleiber; A.A. Mercer; R. Phifer; R.H. Guinter; A.J. Cohen; E.U. Epstein; and M. Narayanan. 1989. "Illness Associated with Child Day Care: A Study of Incidence and Cost," American Journal of Public Health, 79 (4), 479–484.

Bornstein, M.; and Bornstein, H. 1995. "Caregivers' Responsiveness and Cognitive Development in Infants and Toddlers: Theory and Research." In P. L. Mangione (Ed.), Infant/Toddler Caregiving: A Guide to Cognitive Development and Learning. Sacramento: CDE Press.

Bosch, L.; and Sebastián-Gallés. 2001. "Evidence of Early Language Discrimination Abilities in Infants From Bilingual Environments," Infancy, 2 (1), 29-49.

Bruner, J. 1986. Actual Minds, Possible Worlds. Cambridge, MA: Harvard University Press.

Burns, M. R. 1992. A Discourse Analysis of Variation in Children's Language in Preschool, Small Group Settings. Boulder: University of Colorado (doctoral dissertation).

Cross, T.G. 1977. "Mother's Speech Adjustments. The Contribution of Selected Child Listener Variables." In C. E. Snow and C. Ferguson (Eds.), Talking to Children: Language Input and Acquisition, 151-188. Cambridge, MA: Cambridge University Press.

Deuchar, M.; and S. Quay. 2000. Bilingual Acquisition: Theoretical Implications of a Case Study. Oxford: Oxford University Press.

Fantz, R. L. 1958. "Pattern Vision in Young Infants," Psychological Record, 8, 43-47.

Greenspan, S. I. 1981. "Psychopathology and Adaptation in Infancy and Early Childhood: Principles of Clinical Diagnosis and Preventive Intervention," *Clinical Infant Reports*, 1. New York: International Universities Press.

Greenspan, S. I. 1997a. *Developmentally Based Psychotherapy.* Madison, CT: International Universities Press.

Greenspan, S. I. 1997b. *The Growth of the Mind: And the Endangered Origins of Intelligence.* New York: Basic Books.

Greenspan, S. I. 1999. *Building Healthy Minds: The Six Experiences That Create Intelligence and Emotional Growth in Babies and Young Children.* Cambridge, MA: Perseus Publishing.

Greenspan, S. I. 2002. *The Secure Child: Helping Our Children Feel Safe and Confident in an Insecure World.* Cambridge, MA: Perseus Publishing.

Greenspan, S. I.; and S. Shanker. 2003. *The First Idea: How Symbols, Language, and Intelligence Evolved from Primates to Modern Humans.* Cambridge, MA: Da Capo Press.

Greven, J. 1977. *The Protestant Temperament: Patterns of Child-Rearing, Religious Experience, and the Self in Early America.* Chicago: University of Chicago Press.

Hart, B.; and T. R. Risley. 1995. *Meaningful Differences in the Everyday Experience of Young American Children.* Baltimore: Brooks.

Huttenlocher, J. 1984. "Word Perception and Word Production in Children." In D. Bouwhuis and H. Bouma (Eds.), *Attention and Performance: Control of Language Processes,* Vol. X. Hillsdale, NJ: Lawrence Erlbaum Associates.

Johnson, M.; S. Dziurawiec; H. D. Ellis; and J. Morton. 1991. "Newborns' Preferential Tracking of Faces and Its Subsequent Decline," *Cognition*, 40, 1-19.

Klages, M. *Lectures on Jacques Lacan.* Retrieved August 11, 2006 from http://www.colorado.edu/English/courses/ENGL2012Klages/lacan.html.

Kunc, N. 1992. *The Need to Belong: Rediscovering Maslow's Hierarchy of Needs.* Originally published in Villa, R.; J. Thousand; W. Stainback; and S. Stainback, *Restructuring for Caring and Effective Education.* Baltimore, MD: Paul H. Brookes Publishing.

Leboyer, C. 1975. *Birth Without Violence.* New York: Knopf.

Lewis, T.; F. Amini; and R. Lannon. 2000. *A General Theory of Love.* New York: Vintage Books.

Locke, J. 1994. *Great Books in Philosophy: An Essay Concerning Human Understanding.* Amherst, NY: Prometheus Books.

McCune, L.; A. Greenwood; and E.M. Lennon. 2003, April. "Gestures, Grunts, and Words: The Transition to Communicative Competence." Poster session presented at the biennial meeting of the Society for Research in Child Development, Tampa, FL.

Oller, K.; and R. Eilers (Eds.). 2002. *Language and Literacy in Bilingual Children.* Clevedon, UK: Multilingual Matters.

Papou_ek H.; and M. Papou_ek. 1987. "Intuitive Parenting: A Dialectic Counterpart to the Infant's Precocity in Integrative Capacities." In H. F. R. Prechtl (Ed.), *Continuity of Neural Functions from Prenatal to Postnatal Life,* pp. 220-244. Oxford: Spastics International Medical Publications, Blackwell Scientific.

Pearson, B. Z.; and A. M. Navarro. 1998. "Do Early Simultaneous Bilinguals Have a 'Foreign Accent' in One or Both of Their Languages?" In A. Aksu-Koc, E. Erguvanli-Taylan, A. Sumru Ozsoy, and A. Kuntay (Eds.), *Perspectives on Language Acquisition: Selected Papers from the VIIth International Congress for the Study of Child Language,* 156-168. Istanbul: Bogazici University Printhouse.

Piaget, J. 1962. "The Stages of Intellectual Development of the Child." In S. Harrison and J. McDermott (Eds.), *Childhood Psychopathology,* pp. 157–166. New York: International Universities Press.

Program for Infant/Toddler Caregivers. 1988. *Respectfully Yours: Magda Gerber's Approach to Professional Infant/Toddler Care* (video). Sacramento: CDE Press.

Rinaldi, C. 2001. "Reggio Emilia: The Image of the Child and the Child's Environment as a Fundamental Principle." In L. Gandini and C. P. Edwards (Eds.), *Bambini: The Italian Approach to Infant/Toddler Care.* New York: Teachers College Press.

Risley, T. 2005. *Children of the Code Project* (interview). Retrieved August 8, 2006 from http://www.childrenofthecode.org/interviews/risley.htm.

Romaine, S. 1995. *Bilingualism.* Oxford: Blackwell.

Ruopp, R.; J. Travers; F. Glantz; and C. Coelen. 1979. Children at the Center: Final Report of the National Day Care Center Study. Cambridge, MA: ABT Associates.

Schön, D. 1983. The Reflective Practitioner: How Professionals Think in Action. New York: Basic Books.

Shelov, S. 1994. *The American Academy of Pediatrics: Caring for Your Baby and Young Child.* New York: Bantam Books.

Shonkoff, J.; and D. Phillips (Eds.) 2000. *From Neurons to Neighborhoods: The Science of Early Childhood Development,* p. 4. Washington, DC: National Academy Press.

Silber, K. 1965. *Pestalozzi: The Man and His Work,* p. 134. London: Routledge and Kegan Paul.

St. Theophan the Recluse (1998, May/June). Concerning Temptation and Sin (C. Theodorou, Trans.). Orthodox Messenger, The Greek Orthodox Archdiocese of Australia.

Vatican Congregations for the Sacraments and Divine Worship and for the Clergy. March 31, 1977. *A Letter from the Vatican: First Penance, First Communion.* Rome. Retrieved August 10, 2006 from http://www.clerus.org/clerus/dati/1998-12/10-6/First_penance.rtf.html.

Volterra, V.; and R. Taeschner. 1978. "The Acquisition and Development of Language by Bilingual Children," *Journal of Child Language,* 5, 311-326.

About the Contributors

Linda Brault

Linda Brault is the director of BEGINNING TOGETHER, California's Map to Inclusive Child Care, and the First 5 California Special Needs Collaboration and Training Project, all projects of the California Institute on Human Services at Sonoma State University (CIHS-SSU) in collaboration with the Child Development Division of the California Department of Education and First 5 California. Linda is also an instructor in Child Development at MiraCosta Community College. Prior to directing projects for CIHS-SSU, Linda was an early childhood special education teacher for over 18 years. Linda received two Bachelor degrees from the University of the Pacific: one in music therapy and one in psychology. She received her M.A. in special education from CSU Dominguez Hills and holds an Early Intervention Graduate Certificate from San Diego State University.

Carol Brunson Day

Carol Brunson Day is a graduate of the University of Wisconsin, Madison. Dr. Brunson Day completed an M.A. degree in Early Childhood Education at the Erickson Institute of Loyola University in 1970 and a Ph.D. in Education at the Claremont Graduate School in 1979. Dr. Brunson Day is the past President/CEO of the Council for Professional Recognition. She is currently the President of Brunson, Phillips, and Day, Inc. Her work history reflects three years teaching four-year-olds, 14 years teaching college students in human development and early childhood education, and 20 years administering teacher credentialing for personnel working with children age five and younger. Dr. Brunson Day writes, speaks, mentors upcoming leaders, and serves on boards and committees — all with the intent of raising the bar on ensuring the health and well-being of young children and their families.

Amy Laura Dombro

Amy Laura Dombro is the author of numerous articles and books in the areas of parenting, child care, and community mobilization. She received her B.S. in early childhood development and education from the University of Vermont and her M.S. in early childhood education from the Bank Street College of Education. Former head of the Bank Street Infant and Family Center, she consults with a variety of national organizations. One strand of her work is helping initiatives to capture their stories and lessons learned to share with others. Another is to convey information about theory and practice so that it is engaging and easy to apply to real-life situations. Her publications include *Smart Start in Action: Stories of Success from Three Communities* and *The Ordinary Is Extraordinary: How Children Under Three Learn.*

Senta Greene

Senta Greene is founder and chief consultant of Full Circle: A Professional Consulting Agency. She is known at the local, state, and national levels for her leadership and exemplary work including over 16 years of experience in Early Care and Education, Child Life services, and Early Childhood Special Education. She has worked in a variety of settings and capacities, including home and center-based programs in early intervention, Head Starts and Early Head Starts, hospitals, residential settings, county offices of education, and institutes of higher education. She is deeply committed to children and families and actively involved in committees as well as the development of innovative projects such as Jumpstart for Children, California Pre-Kindergarten Learning and Development Curriculum Project, California Department of Education Family Initiative Project, and the California Infant/Toddler Learning and Development Program Guidelines. She has taught both graduate and undergraduate courses for the past eight years at California State University, Northridge, in Special Education and recently in Child and Adolescent Development.

Stanley Greenspan

Dr. Greenspan is clinical professor of Psychiatry and Behavioral Sciences and Pediatrics at George Washington University Medical School, practicing child and adult psychiatrist, supervising child psychoanalyst with the Washington Psychoanalytic Institute, chair for the Interdisciplinary Council on Developmental and Learning Disorders, and co-chair of the Council on Human Development. Dr. Greenspan received his A.B. from Harvard in 1962 and his M.D. from Yale Medical School in 1966. His research centers on the prevention and treatment of emotional and developmental disorders in infants and children. Dr. Greenspan is a founder and past president of the ZERO TO THREE, National Center for Infants, Toddlers and Families; and past chief of the Mental Health Study Center and Clinical Infant Development Program at the National Institute of Mental Health. He has published over 100 articles and chapters and authored or edited over 35 monographs and books. Some of Dr. Greenspan's most recent publications include: *Engaging Autism: The Floortime Approach to Helping Children Relate,*

Communicate and Think, with Serena Wieder; and *Infant and Early Childhood Mental Health,* with Serena Wieder. Dr. Greenspan has received numerous honors, including the American Psychiatric Association's Ittleson Prize for outstanding contributions to Child Psychiatry Research, the American Orthopsychiatric Association's Ittleson Prize for outstanding contributions to American mental health, and the Edward A. Strecker Award for outstanding contributions to American psychiatry.

Deborah Greenwald

Deborah spent 12 years as an infant and toddler caregiver in a variety of center-based settings and currently trains adults in high-quality infant/toddler group care. She holds a B.A. in Child Development from Humboldt State University and an M.A. in Human Development with an emphasis on working with infants and toddlers from Pacific Oaks College. She is a certified Associate of Magda Gerber's Resources for Infant Educarers (RIE), has taught parent-infant guidance classes with Magda at RIE, and is a certified Montessori Infant Toddler Teacher. She is currently a faculty member for the Program for Infant/Toddler Care Training of Trainers Institutes.

Megan Gunnar

Dr. Megan Gunnar is a professor of Child Development at the University of Minnesota. She is the principal investigator for the International Adoption Project, the Family Child Care Research Project, the Peer Relations Project, and the Children's Behavioral Styles Study. Dr. Gunnar received her Ph.D. in Developmental Psychology from Stanford University in 1978. Dr. Gunnar began at the University of Minnesota in the Fall of 1979, becoming a full professor in 1988. In 1996 she was honored as a Distinguished McKnight University Professor. In 2006, she was made a Regents Professor, the highest distinction at the University of Minnesota. Her work documents the importance of sensitive and responsive care by adults in the modulation and buffering of stress physiology in the developing child. Dr. Gunnar is a member of the Society for Research in Child Development, the International Society for Infant Studies, and the International Society of Developmental Psychobiology. She was also a member of the National Academy of Science's panel to review the science of early child development. Dr. Gunnar is currently a fellow of the Canadian Institute of Advanced Research in their program on Experience-based Brain Development, and she serves on the National Scientific Council on the Developing Child.

Janis Keyser

Janis Keyser is a teacher, parent educator, program director, and speaker who specializes in early childhood and family development. She is the coauthor of *Becoming the Parent You Want to Be: A Sourcebook of Strategies for the First Five Years* (www.becomingtheparent.com). She teaches full-time in the Early Childhood Education Department at Cabrillo College in Aptos, California, and has been conducting workshops for parents and teachers for over 35 years. She and her coauthor, Laura Davis, have written Q & A's as parenting experts on iVillage (www.parentsplace.com). She is a nationally recognized speaker at parenting, family, and child development conferences. Janis has her Master's Degree in Human Development from Pacific Oaks College. She is a certified trainer in the Program for Infant Toddler Care (PITC). She is a consultant for WestEd's Family Partnership Initiative project in conjunction with the California State Department of Education. Janis has developed two sets of parenting and teaching videos called *Communication and Positive Discipline* for 2-5 year olds and for school-age children (www.parentingvideos.com). Her new book, *From Parents to Partners: Building Family Centered Care in Early Childhood Programs,* is published by Red Leaf Press.

Anne Kuschner

Anne's current work through the California Institute on Human Services at Sonoma State University include the following: Project Director, Desired Results access Project funded through the Special Education Division, California Department of Education (CDE) to develop a system of child and family outcomes for young children with disabilities; Project Manager for the Continuing Development and Studies to Support Implementation of Desired Results Developmental Profiles – REVISED (DRDP-R) and the CDD/ECE Faculty Initiative Project, both funded through the Child Development Division, CDE. She is also the Project Manager for the ASD: Guidelines for Effective Interventions Project, funded through the Department of Developmental Services. Her background in early childhood special education includes providing technical support and training in areas of inclusion, assessment, program evaluation, and working with families. She has extensive experience in both statewide and national training in developmentally appropriate inclusive practices and has coauthored and co-edited publications disseminated throughout California and nationally.

J. Ronald Lally

Dr. Lally is the Co-Director of the Center for Child and Family Studies at WestEd. He received his doctorate in Educational Psychology from the University of Florida in 1968 and a postdoctoral certificate of Infant Testing from the Child Development Research Centre in London in the same year. He was a professor at Syracuse University and chair of its Department of Child and Family Studies, where he directed the Syracuse University Family Development Research Program. For the past 20 years, he has directed the work of the Program for Infant/Toddler Care (PITC), a collaboration between the California Department of Education and WestEd. The video and print materials of the program are the most widely distributed infant/toddler caregiver training materials in the world. Dr. Lally is on the board of directors and one of the founders of ZERO TO THREE, National Center for Infants, Toddlers and Families. He has served on the Health and Human Services Advisory Committee on Services for Families with Infants and Toddlers that developed Early Head Start, and the National Academy of Science's Head Start Research Roundtable. He was a member of the California Joint Legislative Committee's Master Plan for Education: School Readiness Workgroup, and he has served on California Department of Education's Universal Preschool Blue Ribbon Panel. In 1997 he participated in two

White House conferences, one dealing with brain development and the other with child care. In 2004, he received the California Head Start Association's Founder's Award. His most recent publication is "The Uniqueness of Infancy Demands a Responsive Approach to Care," with Peter L. Mangione in *Young Children*, July 2006.

Claire Lerner

Claire Lerner, L.C.S.W.-C, is a licensed clinical social worker, child development specialist, and Director of Parenting Resources at ZERO TO THREE, where she oversees development of all parenting content, including on its website and in numerous publications. She is also the coauthor of ZERO TO THREE's best-selling parent book, *Learning & Growing Together*. Ms. Lerner writes a regular column in *American Baby Magazine* on young children's behavior. She is frequently quoted in *Parents Magazine, Parenting, Child Magazine*, and *Fit Pregnancy*. In addition, she has been quoted in numerous national daily newspapers such as *The New York Times, Wall Street Journal, USA Today, Los Angeles Times*, the *Boston Globe* and *The London Times*. Ms. Lerner has been a practicing clinician for 20 years, providing parent education and counseling services to families with children of all ages. She also trains early childhood professionals and pediatricians on early childhood development and working effectively with parents. Claire has participated on numerous national advisory panels and task forces related to early child development. She is currently on the Council of the National Parenting Education Network and is a liaison to the American Academy of Pediatrics' Committee on Early Childhood Development.

Alicia Lieberman

Alicia F. Lieberman, Ph.D. is Professor of Psychology and Vice Chair for Academic Affairs at the UCSF Department of Psychiatry, and Director of the Child Trauma Research Project, San Francisco General Hospital. She is also a clinical consultant with the San Francisco Human Services Agency. Born in Paraguay, she received her B.A. from the Hebrew University of Jerusalem and Ph.D. from The Johns Hopkins University. She is on the Board of Directors and President Elect of ZERO TO THREE and on the Professional Advisory Board of the Johnson & Johnson Pediatric Institute. She is the author of *The Emotional Life of the Toddle*, and is also senior author of *Losing a Parent to Death in the Early Years: Treating Traumatic Bereavement in Infancy and Early Childhood*. She lectures extensively in four continents and is a consultant to government agencies and private foundations nationally and abroad. Her major interests include infant mental health, disorders of attachment, child-parent interventions with multiproblem families, and the effects of trauma in the first years of life. Her current research involves treatment outcome evaluation of the efficacy of child-parent psychotherapy with traumatized children aged birth to six. As a triilingual, tricultural Jewish Latina, she has a special interest in cultural issues involving child development, childrearing, and child mental health.

Peter L. Mangione

Dr. Mangione received his Ph.D. in Education and Human Development from the University of Rochester and studied three years as a postdoctoral fellow at the Max-Planck-Institute for Psychiatry in Munich, Germany, where he specialized in infant development and the use of video technology in research on social behavior. He has worked extensively in the fields of child development, early childhood education, research and evaluation design, and public policy. Currently, Dr. Mangione is a Co-Director of WestEd's Center for Child and Family Studies. He provides leadership in the development of a comprehensive training system for infant and toddler caregivers and the evaluation of early childhood programs and services. As a writer, editor, and faculty member, he has made major contributions to the Program for Infant/Toddler Care (PITC), a national model for training early childhood practitioners. He has served as a consulting editor for the *Early Childhood Research Quarterly* and serves on the board of directors of the Child Care Law Center. Recent publications include "The Transition to Elementary School: A Matter of Early Childhood Continuity and Partnerships," in *Elementary School Journal* with T. Speth; and "The Uniqueness of Infancy Demands a Responsive Approach to Care," in *Young Children* with J. Ronald Lally.

Dolores Norton

Dr. Dolores G. Norton has been with the School of Social Service Administration at the University of Chicago since 1976, becoming a Professor with the School of Social Service Administration in 1987. Dr. Norton received her B.A. from Temple University and went on to pursue an M.S.S and a Ph.D. from Bryn Mawr College. In 1996, Dr. Norton was appointed the Samuel Deutsch Chaired Professor in the School of Social Service Administration. Throughout her career, Dr. Norton has served on many boards, which include ZERO TO THREE, The National Center for Infants, Toddlers and Families; Bryn Mawr College Trustee Board and the Bryn Mawr College Board of Advisors to the School of Social Work; Midwest Learning Center for Family Support; Ariel Education Initiative Board; Family Focus Professional Advisory Board; and The Ounce of Prevention Advisory Board. Dr. Norton is also a member of several professional associations including the Society for Research on Child Development. In 1997, the School of Social Service Administration commended Dr. Norton's professorial skills with the Award for Excellence in Teaching.

Jeree Pawl

Jeree Pawl has worked in the area of infant and toddler/caregiver relationships for the past 22 years. She is a clinical professor in the Department of Psychiatry at the University of California, San Francisco, and has been the director of the Infant-Parent Program for 15 years. She is currently on the ZERO TO THREE Board of Directors, and in the past has served as Board President. Dr. Pawl received her B.A. in psychology from the University of Michigan, Ann Arbor, in 1955 and her Ph.D. in psychology from University of Michigan, Ann Arbor, in 1959. Publications include *Learning and Growing Together With Families: Partnering With Parents to Support Young Children's Development,* with Amy Dombro; and *How You Are Is As Important As What You Do,* with Maria St. John.

Carlina Rinaldi

Carlina Rinaldi was a pedagogista and Director of Early Childhood Services in Reggio Emilia, Italy, for 30 years. Currently, she is Executive Consultant to Reggio Children, the International Center for the Defense and Promotion of the Rights and Potential of All Children, and a professor on the Faculty of Science in Early Education at the Universities of Modena and Reggio Emilia. Carlina's educational background includes a degree in Philosophy and Pedagogy from the University of Bologna, Italy, and a Specialization in Psychology from the University of Turin, Italy. Carlina is particularly active in professional development initiatives, lessons, seminars, and research in many countries, carried out in collaboration with the research institutes of European and American universities, including Harvard University's School of Education – Project Zero, Yale University, Mills College, Webster College, Amherst College, University of Chicago, University of Iowa, and University of Colorado at Denver. She coordinated two research projects for Reggio Children: the first in collaboration with Harvard University (Project Zero – Dr. Howard Gardner), the second in collaboration with the University of New Hampshire (Dr. Rebecca New). Carlina also looked after the publication, in 2001, of the book *Making Learning Visible: Children as Individual and Group Learners,* born from the joint research with Harvard Project Zero. Carlina serves as a consultant for professional development and teacher education at Boulder Journey School. She is also consultant to a wide range of companies, including LEGO Company, Sony, IKEA, and ALESSI regarding the field of early childhood education.

Ross Thompson

Dr. Thompson's work focuses on early personality and socioemotional development in the context of close relationships, an interest that contributes to the cross-disciplinary field of developmental relational science. This interest takes his work in two directions. First, his research explores the influence of relational processes on emotional growth, conscience development, emotion regulation, and self-understanding. Recent studies have examined, for example, how the content and structure of early parent-child discourse shapes young children's developing representations of emotion, morality, and self. Second, he has worked on the applications of developmental relational science to public policy problems concerning children and families, such as divorce and child custody, child maltreatment, grandparent visitation rights, and research ethics. Dr. Thompson has served twice as Associate Editor of *Child Development,* was a Senior NIMH Fellow in Law and Psychology at Stanford University in 1989-90, and served on the Committee on Integrating the Science of Early Childhood Development of the National Academy of Sciences (1998-2000). His books include *Preventing Child Maltreatment Through Social Support: A Critical Analysis*

(Sage, 1995), *The Postdivorce Family* (Sage, 1999), and *Toward a Child-Centered, Neighborhood-Based Child Protection System* (Praeger, 2002). He has received the Boyd McCandless Award from the American Psychological Association and the Outstanding Research and Creative Activity Award from the University of Nebraska, where he was also a member of the Academy of Distinguished Teachers.

Louis Torelli

Louis Torelli is the co-founder, with architect Charles Durrett, of Spaces for Children (www.spacesforchildren.com), a child care facility design firm located in Berkeley, California. Louis has worked in the infant/toddler field since 1979, including five years as an infant/toddler caregiver. While working as an infant/toddler caregiver he began to explore the role that the physical environment had on children's learning and development. As a consultant he has designed hundreds of classrooms and childcare facilities, both nationally and internationally. Louis holds a B.A. in Early Childhood Education and a Master of Science from Wheelock College, where he majored in Infant and Toddler Behavior and Development. He is the coauthor of two books: *Landscapes for Learning: Designing Group Care Environments for Infants, Toddlers, and Two-Year-Olds*, with Charles Durrett; and *Educating and Caring for Very Young Children: The Infant/Toddler Curriculum*, with Doris Bergen and Rebecca Reid.

Rebeca Valdivia

Rebeca Valdivia is a Project Director with the Center for Child and Family Studies, WestEd, focusing on the areas of preschool English learners and family partnerships. Prior to coming to WestEd, Rebeca worked with the California Institute on Human Services (CIHS), Sonoma State University, as a Technical Assistance Specialist for various statewide, early childhood projects. Rebeca has also held several leadership positions, including Mentor Teacher, Teacher of the Year at the San Diego County Office of Education, and member of the California Advisory Council on Special Education. Rebeca worked as a bilingual special education teacher and early interventionist for over 15 years, dedicating her bilingual and bicultural skills to serving the Latino community in her various positions. She brings a strong foundation in early childhood development and education with an emphasis on children with disabilities and other special needs and children growing up in dual-language contexts. Rebeca received her B.A. in Diversified Liberal Arts and her M.Ed. in Special Education from the University of San Diego. She received her Ph.D. in Bilingual Education at the University of Illinois, Urbana-Champaign. Rebeca is the proud mother of two sons, who are continuing their journey in becoming balanced bilinguals.

Edward Zigler

Edward Zigler is Sterling Professor of Psychology, Emeritus, at Yale University. He holds a Ph.D. in clinical psychology from the University of Texas at Austin. He was the first Director of the Office of Child Development (now the Administration on Children, Youth, and Families) and Chief of the U.S. Children's Bureau. He was a member of the national planning committees of the Head Start, Follow Thru, and Early Head Start programs. Dr. Zigler founded and is Director, Emeritus, of the Edward Zigler Center in Child Development and Social Policy. He founded the School of the 21st Century model, which has been adopted by more than 1,300 schools in 20 states. Recent publications include *Headstart: The Inside Story of America's Most Successful Educational Experiment;* and *Child Care Choices: Balancing the Needs of Children, Families, and Society.*

Barbara Zurer-Pearson

Barbara Zurer-Pearson has a Masters in Teaching English to Speakers of Other Languages and a Ph.D. in Applied Linguistics from the University of Miami, Florida. While on the faculty of the University of Miami, she was a member of the Bilingualism Study Group (BSG), a multidisciplinary research team that studied developing bilinguals from infants through college students. The team's jointly authored book, *Language and Literacy in Bilingual Children* (Oller & Eilers, Eds.) appeared in 2002. She is currently writing a book for Random House on raising bilingual children. At present, Dr. Pearson is a Research Associate at the University of Massachusetts, Amherst, where she works on the acquisition of African American English. She participated in the development of the Diagnostic Evaluation of Language Variation (DELV), from Harcourt Assessments, Inc., the first standardized language tests normed on African American children. The DELV tests are described in *Seminars in Speech and Language* (February 2004, Seymour & Pearson, Eds.).